TOWARD WIDER ACCEPTANCE OF UN TREATIES

UNITED NATIONS INSTITUTE FOR TRAINING AND RESEARCH

TOWARD WIDER ACCEPTANCE OF UN TREATIES

A UNITAR Study
by Oscar Schachter,
Mahomed Nawaz and John Fried

ARNO PRESS

A Publishing and Library Service of The New York Times

New York   1971

CONTENTS

Chapter Two

ANALYSIS OF STATISTICAL DATA REGARDING ACCEPT-

Chapter Three

INTERNATIONAL MEASURES TO FOSTER ACCEPT-

Chapter Five

CONSTITUTIONAL REQUIREMENTS AND LEGISLATIVE PROCEDURES CONCERNING THE CONCLUSION OF TREATIES

PREFACE

This study, *Toward Wider Acceptance of Multilateral Treaties,* is the first of a series of studies in the field of international law undertaken by UNITAR, in accordance with the decision of the Board of Trustees at its fourth session, held in September 1966. UNITAR's programme of studies in international law has been welcomed by the General Assembly of the United Nations.

The present study was conceived at a discussion by a panel of experts in international law,* which was convened in the summer of 1966 by UNITAR to advise it on a programme of research in international law. In the light of the views expressed by the panel, UNITAR decided to make a systematic inquiry into the several factors hindering acceptance of multilateral treaties and also consider action that might be taken for expediting and fostering the acceptance of such treaties. A research design setting out the objectives, scope and methodology of the project was prepared by the end of 1966 and approved by the UNITAR Board of Trustees at its fifth session, held in March 1967.

This study ascertains empirically to what extent the extrinsic factors, such as constitutional-parliamentary procedures, administrative mechanics, personnel requirements, translation facilities, "final" clauses and others, operate as impediments to acceptance. It also describes to what extent lack of "definitive succession" has impaired the continued application of treaties extended by the predecessor Governments. No attempt has been made in the study, however, to identify the objections by States to the substance of the treaties. The study analyses and

---

* The panel consisted of the following members of the International Law Commission: Messrs. Roberto Ago (Italy), Herbert Briggs (USA), Abdullah El-Erian (UAR), José Maria Ruda (Argentina), Grigory Tunkin (USSR) and Mustafa Kamil Yasseen (Iraq). Others who participated in the discussions were Mr. C. Stavropoulos, Legal Counsel, United Nations, Mr. S. Friedman, Director, Social Science Division (UNESCO) and Mr. O. Schachter, Deputy Executive Director and Director of Research, UNITAR.

describes the range of national and international measures for the wider acceptance of treaties, which include, among others, appeals and exhortation, provision of advisory services and technical assistance, wider dissemination of information, revision of treaties and special national administrative machinery for treaty work.

A variety of sources were used in collecting data for the project, such as United Nations documentation, national legislation and constitutions, legislative debates and other government publications. Information not available in published documentation was gathered from interviews with national and international officials representing various legal systems and geographical regions. A questionnaire (annex I) served as a basis for the interviews and discussions.

A preliminary version of the study was submitted to a panel of national and international officials in December 1968, and the draft was revised subsequently in light of the comments made by the panel. The panel consisted of the following members:

H. E. Mr. Abdullah El-Erian, Ambassador and Deputy Permanent Representative of the United Arab Republic to the United Nations; Mr. Charles Bevans, Assistant Legal Adviser, Treaties Division, Department of State, United States; H. E. Sir Kenneth Bailey, High Commissioner to Canada and the Australian Representative to the Legal Committee of the United Nations since 1946; H. E. Mr. Mustafa Kamil Yasseen, Ambassador and Permanent Representative of Iraq, United Nations Office, Geneva; Mr. Arpad Prandler, Secretary-General of the Association of Jurists, Hungary; Mr. Kamleshwar Das, Division of Human Rights, United Nations Secretariat; Mr. Paul Weis, Office of the United Nations High Commissioner for Refugees, Geneva; Mr. Francisco Urrutia, Office of the United Nations High Commissioner for Refugees, New York.

A paper on Acceptance of Human Rights Treaties (A/CONF.32/15) based on material resulting from this project was submitted to the International Conference on Human Rights held in Teheran in April-May 1968.

The assistance given by national and international officials in the preparation of the study is hereby gratefully acknowledged, as is also the assistance received from the Treaty Section of the Office of Legal Affairs and the Division of Human Rights, United Nations Secretariat.

The study was prepared by Mr. Mahomed Nawaz, with the collaboration of Professor John H. Fried and Mr. Joseph Therattil, under the guidance of Mr. Oscar Schachter.

The Institute as such takes no position on the matters studied under its auspices. It, however, assumes responsibilities for determining whether a study merits publication and dissemination. The views, interpretations and conclusions are those of the authors.

S. O. ADEBO
Executive Director

May 1970

CHAPTER ONE

GENERAL OBSERVATIONS

I. AIM OF THE STUDY

The aim of the study is to investigate causes and factors that delay or prevent acceptance by States of multilateral treaties adopted under United Nations auspices. It is concerned primarily with those impediments to the acceptance of existing—and, by implication, of future—United Nations treaties that could perhaps be reduced by measures taken on the national and international level.

The study, therefore, does not consider objections which States may have to the substance of any international instrument. It inquires into obstacles to acceptance which may be created by non-substantive treaty provisions, and especially into factors that are extraneous to the substance of treaties but result from procedures, personnel matters and the like, that bear upon the conclusion of treaties by States. In these respects, again, the study endeavours to identify factors that may affect acceptance by States generally, or by groups of States, rather than to inquire into the circumstances that may cause a particular State not to adhere to any particular treaty.

MEANING OF THE TERM ACCEPTANCE

The term "acceptance"[1] is used throughout the study in a generic sense, to connote ratification, accession, succession or any other form by which a State expresses its consent to become a party to a treaty.

---

[1] The same terminology was used in the UNITAR study on "Acceptance of Human Rights Treaties," prepared for the International Conference on Human Rights (A/CONF.32/15, 28 March 1968); see also Yuen-li Liang, "Use of the Term 'Acceptance' in United Nations Treaty Practice," *American Journal of International Law,* vol. 44 (1950), pp. 342-349.

Hence, the term also includes "definitive signatures"[2] but excludes signatures that do not contitute definitive consent.

The term "acceptance" covers adherence by signatory States as well as by States that had not participated in the treaty negotiations or had not signed the resulting instrument. The study does, however, make distinctions between these situations when appropriate.

II. THE PROBLEM OF ACCEPTANCE

Although almost all multilateral United Nations treaties have been adopted by very large majorities, and a number of them unanimously or by a nearly unanimous vote, many of them have been accepted by only a minority of States.[3] Non-acceptance or undue delay in acceptance of treaties has deep consequences on the efficacy of codification and the development of international law. These attitudes can retard the entry into force of a treaty,[4] and may even result in the failure of a treaty to come into effect at all.[5] It is noteworthy that according to a provision in the Vienna Convention on the Law of Treaties, 1968, even States that had ratified or acceded to a treaty not yet in force would be freed from the obligation to refrain from acts which would defeat its object and purpose, if the treaty's entry into force is "unduly delayed."[6] Of the 179 multilateral treaties for which the Secretary-General exercises depositary functions, only 138 had entered into force as of mid-June 1968.[7]

Even after a treaty has entered into force, its true effectiveness may be impaired if it applies only to a small number of countries.

---

[2] The Secretary-General stated in his latest Annual Report that between 16 June 1967 and 15 June 1968, the total of 103 signatures newly affixed by Governments to any of the multilateral treaties for which he exercises depositary functions included two "definitive signatures," *Official Records of the General Assembly, 23rd session, Supplement No. 1* (A/7201), p. 206.

[3] See annex II, showing vote on adoption, signatures, acceptances, date of entry into force of 16 selected multilateral treaties; and, generally, chap. two.

[4] To illustrate, the Convention on Fishing, 1958, took nearly eight years; the Convention on the Continental Shelf, 1958, nearly six years; and the Vienna Conventions on Diplomatic and Consular Relations three and four years, respectively, to enter into force.

[5] For examples, see chap. two.

[6] Art. 18 of the Vienna Convention on the Law of Treaties: "A State is obliged to refrain from acts which would defeat the object and purpose of the treaty when . . . (b) it has expressed its consent to be bound by the treaty, pending the entry into force of the treaty and provided that such entry into force is not unduly delayed."

[7] Annual Report of the Secretary-General, *op. cit.,* note 2, p. 206. These figures cover "general" and "limited" international instruments, and include protocols and amendments to, and regulations pursuant to, instruments that themselves had come into effect as of 15 June 1968.

Prompt acceptance by some States may have a positive, and delay by some a negative impact on other States. If a treaty does not receive a sizeable number of acceptances within a reasonable period, States might lose interest in it. For all these and ˋother reasons, prompt acceptance by the widest possible number of States, with the least possible delay, is of crucial significance.

III. DESIRABILITY OF WIDER ACCEPTANCE OF UNITED NATIONS TREATIES

The question, then, of whether speedier and wider acceptance of United Nations treaties is desirable, answers itself; and the study is based on this proposition.

In the United Nations Charter, Member States have set forth specific goals for the world community, which they are pledged to foster. These goals include the promotion of friendly inter-state relations and promotion of the well-being of the individual—a distinction that approximately parallels that between treaties dealing primarily with matters pertaining to inter-state relations, and treaties concerned primarily with the situation of the individual. The dichotomy is rarely if ever complete; and letter and spirit of the Charter enjoin the Organization to concern itself with both, as it views both to be interrelated.[8]

IV. THE SOVEREIGN RIGHT OF STATES TO ACCEPT OR NOT TO ACCEPT A TREATY

Every sovereign State possesses the prerogative to decide whether or not to enter into any international agreement. Hence, except for the very rare cases where a State has entered into an agreement to become a party to a treaty, it is free to exercise this prerogative with respect to any treaty.[9]

However, the problem of acceptance is not exhausted by referring

[8] Yet, the difference in the subject matters of these two categories of treaties cannot be completely disregarded in the context of this study, because: (a) the considerations inducing States to accept, to delay or to reject acceptance may differ for the two categories of treaties; (b) the consequences of limited acceptance may differ for these two categories; (c) different inferences can perhaps be drawn from limited acceptance and even non-acceptance of treaties falling into either category, so that (d) measures on the national and/or international level for the promotion of wider acceptance (or wider informal implementation) may also differ for these two categories of treaties.

[9] However, all States parties to some treaties will be bound by amendments to them if the amendments are ratified by a specified number of States parties. See, for example, Art. 108 of the Charter of the United Nations:

Amendments to the present Charter shall come into force for all Members . . . when they have been . . . ratified . . . by two thirds of

to this undisputed sovereign discretion of States. There exists, in general, no legal obligation to ratify. But, as discussed in chapter three, States members of the International Labour Organisation and of two other specialized agencies have accepted the obligation to put into motion, within specified time limits, their own procedures, with a view to the ratification of certain international instruments.

It has been suggested that even in the absence of such obligations, there still may exist expectations which a State, under the principle of good faith and under considerations of international comity, has to fulfil before it decides to make use of its sovereign right not to ratify. This has been considered applicable when a State has participated in the negotiations leading to the treaty's conclusions or has signed it subject to ratification. In 1930, a League of Nations Committee dealing with these matters stated:[10]

> It is justifiable to assume that the signature of an international convention on behalf of a country indicates an intention on the part of the Government of that country to make a fresh examination of the question with a view of putting the convention into force as far as it is concerned.

The League's experts based this conclusion on the observation that a plenipotentiary who participated in the treaty negotiations

> has by his signature formally approved the convention . . . after having had the opportunity to express the views of his Government and to satisfy himself that the terms of the convention were sufficiently in agreement with his instructions to permit him to give this approval. . . .

and that analogous significance was attributed to a subsequent signature of a treaty because the respective Government "has been able to study the text of the convention in detail"[11] before signing it. The Vienna Convention on the Law of Treaties, mentioned before, adopted the following provision:

> A State is obliged to refrain from acts which would defeat the object and purpose of a treaty when: (a) it has signed the treaty subject to ratification, acceptance or approval until it shall have

---

> the Members . . . including all the permanent members of the Security Council.

Some treaties provide that all parties will be bound by instruments adopted pursuant to provisions of the respective treaty that require only a specific majority vote for adoption, or that all parties will be deemed to have accepted certain instruments so adopted unless they declare the contrary within a specified time limit. These devices aim at reducing the problem of acceptance.

[10] League of Nations, *Report of the Committee appointed to consider the question of ratification and signature of conventions concluded under the auspices of the League of Nations,* 9 May 1930, Doc. A.10. 1930. V, p. 2. For a fuller discussion of this report, see chap. three.

[11] *Ibid.*

made its intention clear that it shall not become a party to the treaty; . . .[12]

The present study, however, concentrates on a point which, as the investigations undertaken during its preparation indicated, is of central importance—namely, that delay in acceptance or non-acceptance often does not result from deliberate decision on the part of Governments but, on the contrary, from circumstances that are extraneous to the substance of the respective United Nations treaties. Such extraneous circumstances delay or prevent acceptance of treaties by Governments that sympathize with or have no specific objection to their objects and purposes, and in fact prevent such States from the exercise of the sovereign prerogative to become parties to the treaties.

V. LEGITIMACY OF THE CONCERN OF INTERNATIONAL ORGANIZATIONS FOR WIDER ACCEPTANCE OF CONVENTIONS CONCLUDED UNDER THEIR AUSPICES

One must also ask at the outset whether, in principle, international organizations have a legitimate concern in the wider acceptance (and full implementation) of treaties concluded under their aegis.

Since the United Nations was created to promote specific aims and purposes, and since treaty law is an indispensable means towards those ends, the Organization is competent, pursuant to its Charter, to adopt treaties, and also, in principle, to be concerned with the fate of those treaties, their entry into force and wider acceptance[13]—even though the adoption of a treaty under United Nations auspices is by itself a significant assertion of the intentions of the international community.[14]

---

[12] See art. 18; the I.L.C. draft art. 15 on the law of treaties went further: according to it the legal obligation "to refrain from acts tending to frustrate the object of [the] proposed treaty" would lie with all States that had participated in the negotiation of the treaty.

[13] The competence of the United Nations is implied in the provisions of Arts. 1, 2, 10, 13, 14, 55, 56, and 62 of the Charter. "The modalities employed in achieving the Purposes and implementing the Principles of the Charter . . . include . . . the drafting and adoption of conventions." (United Nations, *Repertory of United Nations Practice,* vol. 1, 1955, p. 10, para. 12.)

[14] The making of a multilateral United Nations treaty which obtains few acceptances, or for a long time fails to come into effect, need not be an exercise in futility. Depending on its subject matter, such a treaty may influence attitudes and policies of Governments; give impetus to national legislation or the adoption of bilateral treaties; and have an impact on public opinion. Reference could also be made to the right of certain I.L.O. bodies to examine whether Members endeavour to foster standards set by I.L.O. conventions not ratified by them (see chap. three) and to the tendency of some General Assembly resolutions to demand that Members abide by the principles of conventions not ratified by them. (In fact, for example, res. 2332 (XXII) of 18 December 1967 expressed concern about violation of the principles of the International Convention on the Elimination of All Forms of Racial Discrimination, although the Convention was not yet in force.)

This follows not only from legal and empirical logic but is supported by the practice of the Organization, a practice already uncontestedly followed by the League of Nations.

The very decision by an international organ, e.g., the General Assembly, to start upon the making of a multilateral treaty is only taken after deliberations which for some treaties may extend over several years. The decision itself must be considered as a consensus of Members (normally by a very large majority and often unanimously) that the aims to be accomplished by the instrument are desirable. Regularly, both before and after such decision is taken, the Secretariat collects pertinent data and the views of Governments and non-governmental organizations. There is much study and exploratory work by legal experts and experts on the respective substantive matters within individual countries. In the case of codification treaties, the International Law Commission devotes itself to the preparation of drafts, etc. The actual negotiation and formulation of the final text of the convention—whether at special conferences or within the General Assembly—then constitutes both the culmination and renewal of considerable effort on the part of the international organization and of Member States, sometimes extending over years.[15]

Some General Assembly resolutions refer specifically to the appropriateness of concluding certain treaties under United Nations auspices, and link such statements with invitations for speedy and wider acceptance. For example, in resolution 2106 (XX) of 21 December 1965, the Assembly states (a) that "it is appropriate to conclude under the auspices of the United Nations an International Convention on the Elimination of All Forms of Racial Discrimination"[16]; and (b) that it is

---

[15] The General Assembly, in its unanimous res. 2200 (XXI) of 16 December 1966, which adopted and opened for acceptance the two comprehensive covenants on human rights, observed that it had considered the draft Covenants prepared by the Commission on Human Rights "from its 9th regular session," and completed their elaboration "at its 21st session" (preamble, para. 4).

[16] The resolution does not refer to particular provisions of the Charter. The analogous res. 2200A (XXI) regarding the two covenants on human rights, however, refers specifically to Arts. 1, 55 and 56 of the Charter of the United Nations.

See also res. 2461 (XXIII) of 20 December 1968 (adopted by a vote of 78 to 0, with 27 abstentions), wherein the Assembly calls upon the members of the International Monetary Fund "to take the necessary steps for the early ratification and activation of the Special Drawing Rights facility, which is intended to improve the functioning of world economy, including, *inter alia,* the provision of additional resources to developing countries" (preamble, para. 5). The "new facility," the preamble explains, is "to meet the need, as and when it arises, for a supplement to existing reserve assets" (para. 2).

"convinced that the Conventions . . . should be signed and ratified[17] as soon as possible by States" and therefore "invites States" to do so "without delay." More numerous are the Assembly resolutions appealing to States to become parties to United Nations conventions at various intervals after their conclusion—implying, of course, that their conclusion was appropriate in the first place and that the Assembly's concern about their fate is justified.

VI. METHODS USED BY INTERNATIONAL ORGANIZATIONS TO FOSTER ACCEPTANCE OF TREATIES

The legitimacy of the active interest of international organizations in wide acceptance and therefore wide application of treaties made under their auspices is also proven by many precedents. A survey shows that since the beginning of the League of Nations era, international organizations have used a considerable variety of methods and devices to this end.[18] The present study builds upon the fact that this function is, in principle, accepted by the Members and that, as information indicates, greater emphasis by the United Nations on this subject is desired. One purpose of the study is to stimulate discussion of ways and means to increase the extent and efficacy of such efforts.

In its analysis, the study distinguishes between the different approaches that characterize the techniques by which international organizations have endeavoured to foster acceptance of treaties. Making allowance for some rigidity for the sake of emphasis, these approaches can be categorized as follows:

A. the promotional approach;
B. the reporting approach;
C. the servicing approach; and
D. revision of treaties.

A. THE PROMOTIONAL APPROACH

The promotional approach emphasizes exhortation and publicity. It is used in formal appeals and urgings addressed by the General Assembly to States generally; in concentrated campaigns organized under United Nations auspices, such as the International Co-operation Year; in publicity by the Department of Public Information of the United Nations Secretariat; and in co-ordinated activities by non-governmental organizations. Persuasion may also be used by some United Nations bodies with regard to particular instruments, for

---

[17] The reference to signature and ratification is evidently illustrative, rather than exclusive or preferential, as regards the form of acceptance. Art. 18(1) makes clear that "accession" is appropriate, and art. 19(1) shows that all accessions count equally towards reaching the number of 27 parties required to bring the Convention into force. (On these points, see chap. six.)

[18] See chap. three.

example by the United Nations High Commissioner for Refugees with respect to instruments dealing with refugee problems.

B. THE REPORTING APPROACH

If Governments are requested to report to the international organization about steps they have taken or obstacles that have developed regarding the acceptance of treaties, some co-operation is created between the organization and States. This method has been used in particular by the International Labour Organisation; the obligation of its members to transmit specific information on these matters to the I.L.O. was written into the I.L.O. Constitution of 1919, and the extent of the reporting as well as the scrutiny of reports have since been considerably enlarged. Neither the Covenant of the League of Nations nor the Charter of the United Nations established an analogous duty for their Members. But the League requested such reports by a resolution of 1930 regarding all conventions adopted under its aegis. The United Nations has so far made only little use of the device. It would apparently be within the competence of the General Assembly to introduce an analogous procedure either for all or, from time to time, for particular United Nations instruments. In the light of the experience of the I.L.O. Committee of Experts on Application of [I.L.O.] Conventions and Recommendations,[19] consideration could also be given to the establishment of a United Nations committee of experts for the systematic, periodic review of the position of States regarding United Nations treaties,[20] perhaps on the basis of voluntary reporting.

C. THE SERVICING APPROACH

Servicing activities of international organizations with regard to treaties consist in the dissemination of information about United Nations treaties and their status (ratifications, reservations, etc.), in consultations between Government officials and Secretariat officials at Headquarters or at conferences, and in advice from experts in the field, on problems that may stand in the way of adherence by individual States. Certain international technical assistance (provision of legal advisers, training of legal personnel) is also to be mentioned in this connexion.

The study found that elementary technical difficulties—such as uncertainty about the countries that have accepted United Nations treaties and about their reservations, if any, and even unavailability of texts of United Nations treaties and of multilateral and bilateral instru-

---

[19] *Ibid.*

[20] One of the draft resolutions of the International Conference on Human Rights, 1968, recommended establishment of such machinery for human rights treaties. See United Nations, *Final Act of the International Conference on Human Rights,* Teheran, 22 April-13 May 1968 (A/CONF. 32/41), p. 48.

ments superseded or complemented by them—sometimes have delayed or prevented their acceptance. Difficulties resulting from the need for translation of treaties seem to play a relatively small role.

The Secretariats of the United Nations and related agencies are not able to furnish individual Member Governments with authentic interpretations of treaties. However, on request, some agencies provide legally pertinent information, for example, on travaux préparatoires and on practices of other States under the respective treaty, which may assist the inquiring Government to form its own interpretation. Evidence indicates that an extension of this service is desirable, as is the issuing and widest dissemination of authoritative summaries in non-legalistic language of the content and aims of United Nations treaties.

It will be noted that the various efforts by international organizations here summarized differ widely. For example, whereas formal appeals by the General Assembly and other promotional urgings endeavour to stimulate a positive attitude on the part of Governments and public opinion towards acceptances, services such as the dissemination by the secretariat of frequently up-dated information on treaties, and consultations between international and national officials, aim at removing obstacles that may impede even a positive attitude towards a treaty from being translated into action on the national level. The reporting approach, in turn, is more systematic than either the "exhortatory" or "service" approaches. Governments are requested to advise the international organization about the progress towards acceptance which the treaty has made in their countries, and, since this information is regularly to be transmitted within specified time limits, the national authorities concerned are thereby induced to prompt action regarding acceptance. If, in addition, Governments have to account in their reports about the reasons for delays or negative results, this implies in principle that the international organization expects a positive attitude; but this again does not infringe upon States' ultimate discretion to accept or not to accept the treaty, and the requirement is designed to lead to constructive discussion in the competent international body rather than to criticism.

D. Revision of Treaties

If only a few States became parties to a treaty, or if after a certain period of time States not yet parties lose interest in it, it may be because States consider some of the treaty's provisions as too exacting or no longer adequate. Under such circumstances, the international organization concerned has sometimes proceeded to revise the instrument or to adopt an additional one. Analysis shows that this has in some cases been successful.[21] The 1930 report of the League of Nations Committee, mentioned

---

[21] See chap. three, sec. IV.

before, recommended that every future general convention of the League of Nations should provide that, unless a certain number of States were bound by it after a certain period, a meeting of the signatories should be held to consider among other things its amendment.[22]

Finally, the study lists certain other devices that have been inserted into some treaties to foster their acceptance. For example, a treaty may state that certain of its provisions are alterable by special agreements; or that certain rights or advantages may be reserved to States parties to it, and the like. Such devices have been used only in the case of some treaties but could, if appropriate, be written into certain future instruments.

VII. METHODOLOGY OF THE STUDY

A. Statistical Analysis of 81 United Nations Treaties

The study is based on a statistical analysis of the acceptance record of United Nations treaties. This statistical analysis concentrates on 55 general multilateral instruments adopted under the auspices of the United Nations (or adopted under the auspices of the League of Nations and subsequently "taken over" by the United Nations) and all 26 treaties adopted by the United Nations Economic Commission for Europe (E.C.E.), the latter being known as "limited" multilateral treaties.[23] For the sake of simplicity, all 81 treaties are here referred to as "United Nations treaties."

1. Selection and subject matters of the 81 treaties

As mentioned before, the Secretary-General of the United Nations performs depositary functions in regard to 179 multilateral treaties.[24] The figure of 81 was reached by including all United Nations treaties on a wide variety of subjects, and by omitting therefore, in the main, constitutional instruments of international organizations, GATT treaties, some treaties adopted by the League of Nations and protocols adopted by the General Assembly to amend certain League treaties.

The subject matters of the 55 general multilateral treaties covered

---

[22] League of Nations, *op. cit.*, note 10, p. 6.

[23] The term "general" multilateral treaties refers to treaties to which all Members of the United Nations and often certain other States can become parties. The term "limited" multilateral treaties refers to treaties to which only a limited number of States can become parties; namely, in the case of the 26 E.C.E. treaties, the Members of the E.C.E. and, as stipulated in these treaties, sometimes other States. For a fuller discussion of the States eligible to accept general and limited United Nations treaties, see chap. two. Where appropriate, the study also refers to treaties other than these 81, adopted under the auspices of the United Nations or a related agency; for example, the International Labour Organisation.

[24] Annual Report of the Secretary-General, *op. cit.*, note 2, p. 206.

by the statistical analysis include the law of the sea, diplomatic and consular relations, various aspects of human rights, transport and communication, education, narcotic drugs, international commercial arbitration
and pacific settlement of disputes; the 26 E.C.E treaties pertain mainly
to transportation, communication and inland navigation.

2. *Evaluation of statistical data regarding acceptance of United*
Nations treaties

In evaluating the statistical data here presented, several factors are
to be taken into consideration:

(a) Inclusion of some international treaties with a relatively high or
fast record of acceptances[25] or exclusion of some with a low record[26]
would have "inflated" the statistical picture and thus made it more
"optimistic"; and inclusion of others of recent date[27] would have "wors-
ened" the picture and thus made it more "pessimistic."

(b) The study does not weigh the statistical data according to the
relative importance of the instruments. Weighing them would have
introduced an element of arbitrariness, although their uneven importance
is fully recognized. However, chapter two also presents statistical data on
the acceptance record of certain types of United Nations treaties as well
as on categories of States.[28]

(c) The large number of newly independent States increases the
statistical significance of treaties that had been extended to their territories by the predecessor Governments. The statistical data here given
include only those treaties in this category regarding which the "new"
States have specifically notified the Secretary-General that they have
accepted them through succession.[29] These notifications and therefore the
statistical acceptance figures based on them are incomplete, because some
"new" States have not yet reached a decision or have not yet notified the
Secretary-General of their decision with respect to all such "old" United
Nations treaties, and their eventual notification may reveal that they wish
to be parties from the date of independence or as of a date prior to the
end of 1968.

[25] Such as the Convention on the Privileges and Immunities of the
United Nations, 1946, which, as of 31 December 1968, received 99
acceptances.

[26] For example, the Optional Protocols concerning Settlement of Disputes to the Vienna Convention on Diplomatic Relations, 1961, Consular
Relations, 1963, and the Law of the Sea, 1958.

[27] For example, the International Coffee Agreement and the new
Convention on Road Traffic, which were opened for signature on 18 March
1968 and 8 November 1968, respectively.

[28] See also annexes II and III.

[29] Examination of Devolution Agreements between "new" States and
States previously responsible for their international relations indicated that
some of those agreements do not specify the treaties covered by them.

This statistical inexactness mirrors the much more significant fact that there exists a grey area of uncertainty about the validity of a number of treaties for a considerable number of States—an uncertainty which Devolution Agreements intended to prevent, and which should be removed.

(d) The study is generally cautious in suggesting correlations between constitutional or administrative practices of States and their acceptance of United Nations treaties or, in turn, between certain "final" clauses of such treaties and the number of States parties to them. But on some points it seemed permissible to draw inferences from the statistical analysis concerning obstacles to adherence. Conversely, it may also be noted that the statistical data do not support some widely held views about the adverse effect of certain factors upon the acceptance prospects of United Nations treaties.

(e) Some of the United Nations instruments covered in these statistics clarify, concretize and elaborate upon pre-existing customary international law or general principles of international law. States which have failed to accede to a particular humanitarian convention, for example, cannot be presumed to deny the prohibition of the anti-humanitarian acts defined in the convention and would not claim that such acts are not proscribed by general international law or are permissible under their domestic law.

The study found that considerations of this nature may also cause Governments to view as not urgent their adherence to United Nations conventions that concretize previous United Nations declarations on the same subject.

B. Information About Extraneous Factors Impeding Wider Acceptance

Evidently, the acceptance statistics of treaties do not indicate factors affecting acceptance that are extraneous to the content of those treaties. However, an essential task of the study consisted in analyzing extraneous factors that may prevent competent and timely examination of treaties: for example, uncertainties about the portent of a convention that cause it to be rejected or. shelved indefinitely, or administrative difficulties that make the examination of an international instrument so formidable an undertaking as to dim the chances of that examination.

Information about such extraneous factors was obtained through interviews with representatives of Members, legal advisers, United Nations officials familiar with those matters, United Nations experts who had gained experience in the field and other competent sources. This information and the inferences drawn from it are not precise. Yet, the availability of knowledgeable persons from many States yielded valuable insights.

The over-all conclusion drawn from this type of information is that non-acceptance or indefinite delay of acceptance is frequently caused by factors that have nothing to do with the substance of the treaties involved, or which do not imply disagreement with the treaties' aims. These factors prevent or adversely affect the very examination of United Nations treaties, and they merit remedial action on the international and national levels.

VIII. THE IMPORTANCE OF WIDER ADHERENCE TO UNITED NATIONS TREATIES FOR THE ACCOMPLISHMENT OF THE PURPOSES OF THE UNITED NATIONS

Some dissatisfaction can be discerned regarding the relatively slow development of international law through treaties. Such an attitude in itself forms an obstacle, however intangible, to wider acceptance of United Nations treaties.

In this connexion, reference should be made to the fact that the General Assembly has used devices other than treaties in order to promote the aims of the United Nations. Such devices include resolutions declaratory of international law; the creation of United Nations bodies for the performance of particular functions;[30] and declarations of the General Assembly. These devices do not require specific ratification or accession by States.

However, these devices do not diminish the importance of treaties. This is especially evidenced by the fact that the General Assembly has found it necessary to adopt formal conventions on subjects for which it had laid down general principles in declarations. For example, in addition to the Universal Declaration of Human Rights, it adopted the two international Covenants on human rights, as well as the Declaration on the Elimination of all Forms of Racial Discrimination and a convention on that subject.[31]

---

[30] For example, UNICEF and UNWRA. Sometimes the General Assembly uses the institution-making power (power to establish "subsidiary organs") bestowed on it by Art. 22 of the Charter to pursue some of the goals of a convention that, for lack of ratifications, failed to enter into force. The United Nations Conference on Trade and Development (UNCTAD), established by res. 1995 (XIX) of 30 December 1964, may be considered as fulfilling some of the functions envisaged for the International Trade Organization (ITO), the constitution of which (Havana Charter of 24 March 1968) never entered into force.
The *Repertory of United Nations Practice* (vol. I, pp. 730-739 and Supplement I, pp. 230-237) lists 109 subsidiary organs established by the General Assembly during its first ten sessions alone.

[31] In his address at the International Conference on Human Rights, Teheran, 1968, the Secretary-General stated that United Nations Conventions and Declarations on human rights have established "a body of principles and legal rules . . . [which] constitute . . . a rapidly developing branch of international law":
The adoption of the Universal Declaration was followed by the approval [by the General Assembly] of a number of other United

Characteristically, the International Conference on Human Rights, Teheran, 1968—which, as the Secretary-General pointed out at its opening, was to propose "new ways" for the promotion of human rights—variously urged States to ratify or accede to international conventions.[32] In fact, it called upon the General Assembly "to take steps in order to ensure . . . the widest possible accession" to instruments relating to human rights. The resolution XXII of the Teheran Conference is exclusively devoted to the topic of Universal Accession by States to International Instruments relating to Human Rights:

> The International Conference on Human Rights,
> Noting that the United Nations has adopted a considerable number of multilateral international instruments designed to promote the observance and protection of human rights for signature and ratification or accession by States,
> Considering that for the universal and truly effective implementation and protection of human rights it is essential to secure the widest possible participation in international instruments relating to human rights, . . .
> 1. Invites the States to consider their participation in international instruments relating to human rights with a view to their accession to as many of them as possible;
> 2. Calls upon the United Nations General Assembly to take steps in order to ensure the principle of universality of human rights and the widest possible accession to such instruments.

The conviction of the international community that treaties are indispensable for the achievement of its goals is expressed in the International Covenant on Economic, Social and Cultural Rights, unanimously adopted by the General Assembly on 16 December 1966:

> Art. 23. The States Parties to the present Covenant agree that

---

Nations Declarations and Conventions which . . . progressively led to the building of principles and legal rules for the conduct of those whose responsibility is to ensure respect for human dignity. These principles and rules constitute now a rapidly developing branch of international law which the United Nations elaborated. (A/CONF.32/41 at p. 35.)

[32] See especially the Conference's res. VI, para. 5, regarding the Convention on Racial Discrimination "and other conventions directed against discrimination in the field of employment and education"; res. V, para. 1, regarding the Convention on Racial Discrimination; res. IX, para. 4, regarding five United Nations conventions, two I.L.O. conventions and one UNESCO convention; res. XIII, para. 2, urging States to "accede to the international instruments dealing with the protection of the rights of refugees and especially" the Refugee Convention, 1951, and the Refugee Protocol, 1967; res. XXI, regarding the two International Covenants on human rights, 1966; res. XXIII, regarding the Hague Conventions of 1899 and 1907, the Geneva Protocol of 1925 prohibiting the use of "asphyxiating, poisonous or other gases and of all analogous liquids, materials and devices," and the Red Cross (Geneva) Conventions of 1949.

international action for the achievement of the rights recognized in the present Covenant includes such methods as the conclusion of conventions, the adoption of recommendations, the furnishing of technical assistance and the holding of regional meetings and technical meetings for the purpose of consultation and study . . .[33]

Increasing Importance in the Future

As the previously mentioned 1930 report of the League of Nations shows, the problem of acceptance of international instruments existed even four decades ago. Since then, it has become more difficult because of the increased number of States; because of the increased number and complexity of subjects requiring international regulation and of legal instruments requiring the attention of Governments and other national authorities; and because of the special situation of newly independent and developing States.

However, the awareness of the need to overcome these problems has also increased. As the United Nations is called upon to deal with new questions raised by the development of technology and requiring multilateral treaties—for example, the use of outer space, the utilization of the resources of the sea bed, the prevention of pollution—ways and means to obtain wider acceptance of United Nations conventions become ever more urgent.

---

[33] The opinion of the General Assembly that the application of existing and the creation of additional treaties are paramount among the methods to be used to attain goals of the international community is also illustrated, for example, by its invitation to the Secretary-General "to study (a) steps which could be taken to ensure the better application of existing humanitarian conventions and rules in all armed conflicts"; and "(b) the need for additional humanitarian international conventions or for other appropriate legal instruments to ensure the better protection of civilians, prisoners and combatants in all armed conflicts and the prohibition and limitation of the use of certain methods and means of warfare" (res. 2444 (XXIII), unanimously adopted on 19 December 1968).

CHAPTER TWO

ANALYSIS OF STATISTICAL DATA REGARDING ACCEPTANCE OF UNITED NATIONS TREATIES

I. STATISTICAL DATA*

A. Statistics About General Multilateral Treaties

Annex II to this study presents data on the following aspects of 16 selected United Nations treaties: date of adoption, vote on adoption, date of entry into force,[1] number of States that have become parties and number of States whose signatures have not been followed by ratification. Annex III shows, in the form of a chart, treaty by treaty for each of the 55 instruments covered in the study,[2] the number and names of States that have become parties, or are still only signatories. In turn, it shows State by State for each of the eligible 132 States (see below) to which of those 55 instruments they have become parties, and which they signed but have not yet ratified.

Annex IV indicates the sources of the texts of the "general" multilateral treaties, as well as the abbreviations of titles of treaties used in this study.

---

* All the statistics in this chapter, as in this study, are as of 31 December 1968.

[1] Annex II thus indicates the time required for each of the 16 multilateral treaties to obtain the number of acceptances necessary to enter into force. The interval between deposition of the last such instrument and the treaty's coming into force must, however, be taken into consideration. Regarding the tempo of acceptance in general of various United Nations treaties, see sec. IV of this chapter.

[2] The subject matters of the treaties included in this study cover the law of the sea, diplomatic and consular relations, human rights, education, transport and communication, narcotic drugs, enforcement of arbitral awards and the pacific settlement of disputes.

In presenting the acceptance figures for each treaty and each State, these statistics also indicate the over-all adherence to those instruments, the relative popularity of United Nations treaties on different subject matters and the gaps between signature and ratification. In conjunction with the United Nations records of notifications by "new" States of their succession to treaties that had been extended to their territories by the predecessor Governments, the statistics also shed some light on the role of succession as a means of acceptance.

1. Over-all extent of acceptances (ratifications, accessions and successions)

As of 31 December 1967, the 55 "general" multilateral treaties had received an over-all total of 1,963 acceptances; that is, about 27 percent of the maximum attainable number of acceptances by 132 States, being the aggregate of 123[3] Member States of the United Nations and 9[4] other States. During the next calendar year, these treaties received altogether 120 additional acceptances, so that by 31 December 1968, the over-all total stood at 2,083 and the over-all aggregate at about 28 percent. This total includes acceptance records of the more recent treaties, such as the two international covenants on human rights (adopted on 16 December 1966). If these covenants and other treaties concluded since 1 January 1966 are excluded from the computation, the aggregate over-all acceptance record of the remaining treaties would be about 30 percent.

2. Over-all extent of signatures not followed by ratifications

The total number of signatures not followed by ratifications as of 31 December 1968 was 586. Were all of these signatures followed by ratifications, the aggregate of acceptances by the 132 States of the 55 instruments would rise to about 37 percent of its maximum, as against the figure of about 28 percent mentioned above. This shows a 9 percent gap between the signatures and ratifications. But it also shows that the 28 percent record of acceptances does not represent the full spectrum of the interest of States in these treaties.

3. Extent of succession

Of the 2,083 acceptances, 234 were notified by "new" States[5] as

---

[3] Mauritius, Equatorial Guinea and Swaziland, which became Members of the United Nations after 1 January 1968, are not included in this figure.

[4] Federal Republic of Germany, Holy See, Liechtenstein, Monaco, Republic of Korea, San Marino, Switzerland, Republic of Vietnam and Western Samoa.

[5] All members of the League of Nations (including certain Members of the Commonwealth), as well as all States not members of the League that were independent before 1945, are herein considered "old" States. By this criterion, of the 132 States covered by these statistics, 71 are "old" States and 61 "new" States.

succession to treaties extended to their territories by predecessor Governments. About 50 of the 55 treaties here discussed have been succeeded to by some newly independent State or States. Yet, the over-all aggregate of express notifications by the 61 "new" States of succession to "old" treaties is far short of the number that would be possible. It is to be investigated to what extent the failure of "new" States to give notification of succession or to accede formally to "old" treaties has resulted in their not being listed as parties to treaties that were extended to their territories by the predecessor Governments. (See chap. seven.)

B. STATISTICS ABOUT LIMITED MULTILATERAL TREATIES (treaties adopted under the auspices of the Economic Commission for Europe)

Twenty-six "limited" multilateral treaties have been adopted under the auspices of the Economic Commission for Europe (E.C.E.).[6] They deal *inter alia* with transportation, communication and inland navigation matters. As of 31 December 1968, the over-all total of acceptances of these 26 treaties by the 31 Member States of the E.C.E., plus Switzerland, which has a consultative position in the work of the Commission, was 278[7] or about 34 percent, compared with the 28 percent aggregate of the "general" multilateral treaties.

To what extent the relatively simpler acceptance procedures of E.C.E. treaties have contributed to their speedier and wider acceptance is examined in chapter VI.

II. ANALYSIS OF ACCEPTANCE PATTERNS OF CERTAIN CATEGORIES OF STATES REGARDING GENERAL MULTILATERAL TREATIES

Since statistics in themselves do not disclose the reasons for which States delay acceptance of treaties or fail to accept them, no attempt will be made in this chapter to identify the possible causes. However, if the acceptance figures of the 55 general multilateral treaties are grouped according to certain categories of States, and the data of each group statistically analysed, some objectively different patterns of behaviour regarding acceptance are discernible. These indications may permit some hypotheses about possible causes of delay in acceptance or non-acceptance of treaties. For the purposes of statistical analysis, the

[6] The E.C.E. treaties and the number of European States parties to them are enumerated in annex V to this study.

[7] The E.C.E. treaties are also open to Member States of the United Nations, who may be admitted in consultative capacity to take part in the work of the E.C.E. Their acceptances are not included in the figure of 278. Were they to be included, the aggregate percentage of acceptance would be higher than the 34 percent.

following categories of States have been chosen: "new" and "old" States; "small" States; Latin American States; Eastern and Western European States.

A. "NEW" STATES

The total record of acceptances by the new States[8] of all the general multilateral treaties is about half that of the old States. In quantitative terms, the aggregate of the new States is about 21 percent, and that of the old States about 40 percent. Four new States which have attained independence since 1960 have so far not accepted any of the 55 treaties; 4 have accepted one each; and 5 have accepted two each. The acceptance record of some States which have gained independence since 1945 is considerably better, but it is still true that most of the States which have accepted more than half of the 55 treaties are old States.

Although it has been shown above that the over-all aggregate of successions to treaties has been relatively low, succession has been a factor in facilitating wider acceptance by some of the new States of the old treaties. The new States that are listed as parties to more than 20 treaties are generally those that notified succession to treaties extended to their territories by the predecessor Governments.[9]

B. "SMALL" STATES

States with a population of less than one million, and/or a small territory, are referred to as small States for the purposes of this analysis. The acceptance records of States which are small in these terms are found to be comparatively low. In statistical terms, the over-all aggregate of 18 such States[10] is about 15 percent, or approximately half of the world level. Three of the small States have so far not accepted any of the 55 treaties, 2 have accepted only one, and 2 have adhered to only two. Some of these States are not only small but also very new. This seems to indicate that some small States, especially the newly independent ones, are faced with problems of their own. What these problems are calls for inquiry.[11]

---

[8] For the definition of this category of States, see note 5 above.

[9] For example, 10 of the 27 acceptances by Ghana are through succession; so are 18 of the 26 acceptances by Jamaica, 16 of the 23 acceptances by Nigeria, 19 of the 26 acceptances by Sierra Leone and 19 of the 27 acceptances by Trinidad and Tobago. See also chap. seven.

[10] Barbados, Botswana, Cyprus, Gabon, Gambia, Guyana, Holy See, Iceland, Lesotho, Liechtenstein, Luxembourg, Maldive Islands, Malta, Monaco, San Marino, Trinidad and Tobago and Western Samoa have populations under one million. Singapore, with a population close to two million, has a territory of about 581 sq. km.

[11] See chap. four on National Administrative Machinery, which refers, *inter alia,* to personnel and other administration problems in small States.

C. LATIN AMERICAN STATES

The over-all record of acceptance by the Latin American States, excluding the Caribbean countries, is about 23 percent, slightly above that of the new States. A salient feature in the acceptance pattern of some Latin American States is that the proportion of signatures not yet followed by ratifications is much higher than it is at the world level. Of the 586 such signatures at the world level, 166 or about 28 percent are from the Latin American States. To illustrate: one has signed 21 general United Nations treaties but has ratified only 3 of them. Another has signed 7 but has not ratified any of them.[12] Yet another, with a relatively high record of acceptances among the Latin American States, has become a party to 16 treaties, but signatures of 15 others are still pending. Whether constitutional and legislative procedures regarding the conclusion of treaties create obstacles to speedier ratification calls for inquiry.[13]

D. EASTERN AND WESTERN EUROPEAN STATES

In the aggregate, the record of acceptances by the Eastern European States of the general multilateral treaties is about 40 percent. That of the Western European States is approximately the same. But one difference in the acceptance pattern of the Eastern and Western European States is shown by the statistics, namely, comparatively fewer signatures have not been followed by ratifications in the Eastern European States. With respect to the 55 treaties, there were only 28 such signatures by the end of 1968. Most of them were for the more recent treaties, namely, the Conventions on Racial Discrimination, 1965, and on Transit Trade of Land-Locked States, 1965, and the two Covenants on Human Rights, 1966. Pending signatures by Western European countries totalled 163 as of 31 December 1968. Although the number of Western European Members of the United Nations considerably exceeds that of the Eastern European Members, the proportion of unratified signatures is much higher in the former. To what extent constitutional and legislative procedures bear on this phenomenon calls for inquiry.[14]

III. ANALYSIS OF ACCEPTANCE STATISTICS IN TERMS OF TYPES AND TOPICS OF TREATIES

A. TREATIES ON THE LAW OF THE SEA, DIPLOMATIC AND CONSULAR RELATIONS

There are four conventions on the law of the sea, 1958, one on diplomatic relations, 1961, and another on consular relations, 1963.[15] An

---

[12] This country has acceded to one treaty, however.

[13] See chap. five.

[14] *Ibid.*

[15] All these conventions arose from the work of the International Law Commission. The four treaties on the law of the sea deal with the Territorial Sea, the High Seas, Fishing and the Continental Shelf, respectively.

optional protocol concerning the Compulsory Settlement of Disputes supplements the conventions on the law of the sea. The conventions on diplomatic and consular relations are each supplemented by two optional protocols, one concerning Acquisition of Nationality, another concerning the Compulsory Settlement of Disputes.

These treaties, which clarify, solidify and elaborate upon pre-existing customary international law, differ from one another in scope and substance.

The Convention on Diplomatic Relations is in a class of its own. It differs from the law of the sea conventions insofar as it deals with matters which occupy a large part of the business of Foreign Offices or the Ministries of External Affairs. It differs from the Convention on Consular Relations insofar as its subject matters are not regulated by bilateral treaties to the same extent as are consular relations. The treaties on the law of the sea, in turn, differ from one another. In particular, the Convention on the Continental Shelf deals with a topic that has come into prominence since the Second World War; and the Convention on Fishing and Conservation of Living Resources of the High Seas is probably the "most controversial" of all four conventions.

The acceptance statistics of these six treaties will be reviewed briefly. Of the four law of the sea treaties, the Convention on the High Seas has received the largest number of acceptances, with 43, and the Convention on Fishing and Conservation of the Living Resources the lowest, 27. The two other treaties have received 36 and 39 acceptances, respectively.

Of the 132 States here considered, 26 are land-locked, and 106 are maritime States. The over-all record of acceptance by the latter States of the four law of the sea conventions is about 34 percent, and that of the land-locked States is about 26 percent. The Convention on the Continental Shelf scored lowest among the land-locked States (5 acceptances), and the Convention on the High Seas scored highest (10 acceptances).

Additionally, the Conventions on the Territorial Sea, the High Seas, Fishing and the Continental Shelf have received 23, 23, 23 and 24 unratified signatures, respectively.

Of the six above conventions, the Convention on Diplomatic Relations, 1961, has received the largest number of acceptances—82. Of the 61 new States, 35 have become parties to it; and of the 71 old States, 47. The proportion is therefore about 55 percent of the new and 66 percent of the old States.

Thirty-three States have become parties to the Vienna Convention on Consular Relations, 1963; in addition, there are 36 signatures pending ratification. Comparatively, it has made less strides than the Vienna Convention on Diplomatic Relations. The proportion of acceptances by the new States and old States is about the same—24 percent.

B. TREATIES RELATING TO THE SETTLEMENT OF DISPUTES

The four general multilateral instruments in this group include the Revised General Act for the Pacific Settlement of Disputes and three Optional Protocols concerning the Compulsory Settlement of Disputes (Vienna Convention on Diplomatic Relations, Vienna Convention on Consular Relations and the Conventions on the law of the sea).

Of these, the Revised General Act, although adopted in 1949, shows the smallest number of acceptances—6. The Optional Protocol regarding the Convention on Diplomatic Relations has received 33 acceptances; that related to the law of the sea Conventions, 21; and that related to the Convention on Consular Relations, 11. Thus, all three Optional Protocols concerning the Compulsory Settlement of Disputes lag far behind the respective substantive treaties; in fact, the Convention on Diplomatic Relations has received more than double, and the Convention on Consular Relations three times, the number of acceptances of the respective Optional Protocols.

The proportion of new and old States that have become parties to the three Optional Protocols is as follows: 11 percent of the new and 20 percent of the old States for the Protocol on the law of the sea Conventions; 21 percent new and 28 percent old States for the one relating to the Convention on Diplomatic Relations; and 10 percent new and 7 percent old for the one relating to the Convention on Consular Relations.

C. HUMAN RIGHTS TREATIES

The statistical survey covers the 20 United Nations human rights treaties, whose subjects include genocide, slavery, refugees, statelessness, traffic in persons, political rights of women, elimination of racial discrimination and, broadly, the economic, social, cultural, civil and political rights of the individual.[16] In terms of their dates of adoption and their scope, the treaties differ among themselves—apart from the fact that human rights treaties differ from most other treaties by primarily referring to individuals rather than to inter-state relationships. Some of the human rights treaties, for example those on slavery and traffic in women, deal with matters which have been subject to international regulations long before the creation of the United Nations. Others, such as the Covenant on Civil and Political Rights and the Convention on Racial Discrimination, cover topics which have traditionally been regulated by internal

---

[16] Some conventions adopted under the auspices of the I.L.O., especially on forced labour, freedom of association and non-discrimination, as well as the UNESCO Agreement on Non-Discrimination in Education, are sometimes also referred to as human rights treaties in United Nations terminology. They are not included in the statistics here presented but are mentioned in this study when appropriate.

rather than international law. Furthermore, whereas the earlier human rights treaties on slavery and traffic in women generally confined themselves to requiring States to inform each other of the laws adopted to implement them, the more recent ones, for example the Covenant on Civil and Political Rights, 1966, and the Convention on Racial Discrimination, 1965, set up implementation machinery on the international plane.

Two of the human rights treaties, the Supplementary Slavery Convention of 1956 and the Genocide Convention of 1948, may be singled out for comment. Both embody humanitarian and moral concepts that are universally recognised, and both declare violations of these concepts to be offences punishable by the national law. Under the Genocide Convention, however, any Contracting Party can call upon United Nations organs to intervene. Both treaties have so far received 73 acceptances.[17] If, however, the acceptance records of the new and old States are compared, differences appear: of 61 new States, 18 (30 percent) have become parties to the Genocide Convention and 28 (46 percent) to the Supplementary Slavery Convention; and of 71 old States, 55 (77 percent) have accepted the former and 45 (63 percent) the latter.

Of the three treaties dealing with various aspects of the Status of Women, the Convention on the Political Rights of Women, 1952, is, with 61 acceptances, by far the most popular, although some federal States have encountered difficulties in acceding to it.[18] The Convention on the Nationality of Married Women, 1957, ranks second, with 41 acceptances, while the Convention on Consent to Marriage, Minimum Age for Marriage and Registration of Marriages, 1962—topics traditionally regulated in many countries by custom and religion—lags behind with 18 acceptances.

Distinguishing again between the aggregate acceptance record of the new and old States, we find that 34 percent of the new and 56 percent of the old States have become parties to the Convention on the Political Rights of Women. The analogous proportions are 20 percent to 39 percent for the Convention on the Nationality of Married Women and 10 percent to 17 percent for the Convention on Consent to Marriage, etc.

Of the two treaties dealing with the status of refugees, the Convention of 1951 has been accepted by 54 States and the Protocol of 1967 by 28 States.[19] The 54 acceptances of the Convention include 15 successions, mostly from the newly independent States of Africa.

---

[17] The number of signatures not yet ratified—6 and 5, respectively—is also virtually identical.

[18] See chap. five.

[19] Regarding the restricted applicability of the Convention of 1951 and the manner in which the Protocol of 1967 removing these restrictions was adopted, see chap. three.

Two treaties deal with statelessness. The Convention on Stateless Persons, 1954, in essence requires contracting countries to treat such persons in certain respects (acquisition of property, gainful employment, etc.) at least as favorably as they treat aliens, and in certain other respects (exercise of religion, access to the Courts, elementary education, social security, etc.), at least as favourably as they treat their own nationals. But the 1954 Convention contains no specific obligations with regard to citizenship questions—topics usually not dealt with in international treaties.[20] The Convention entered into force on 6 June 1959, after receiving the required 6 ratifications or accessions, and has since been accepted by 13 additional States.

In turn, the Convention on the Reduction of Statelessness, adopted on 30 August 1961, focuses on citizenship questions; it obliges contracting parties to grant citizenship to stateless persons under specified conditions. Seventeen years after its acceptance, this treaty had been accepted by only one State, so that its chances of ever entering into force are very dim.[21] It may be observed, however, that the 1954 Convention on Stateless Persons has received only about one third the number of acceptances (19) of the 1951 Refugee Convention (54) to which it bears resemblance.

Another treaty that has fared poorly is the Convention on the International Right of Correction, 1953. Almost 16 years after its adoption, only 8 States have adhered to it. This Convention enables States parties to correct false news dispatched from abroad by bringing the error to the attention of the receiving State party, which is then bound to release the communiqué to the correspondents in its territory. However, no obligation is imposed on the press or other media of information to publish the communiqué.[22]

Of the three more recent human rights treaties—the International Convention on the Elimination of all Forms of Racial Discrimination, 1965, the International Covenant on Civil and Political Rights and the International Covenant on Economic, Social and Cultural Rights, 1966—the first has received 27 acceptances and the two others one acceptance each. In addition, they have received 48, 37 and 38 unratified signatures, respectively. As indicated earlier, these treaties differ significantly in scope from other human rights instruments. By the end of 1968, 13

---

[20] It merely provides that "the Contracting States shall as far as possible facilitate the assimilation and naturalisation of stateless person. . ." (art. 32).

[21] The Convention is to enter into force two years after the date of deposit of the sixth acceptance (art. 18, (1)).

[22] It took over nine years to obtain the six acceptances required to put this Convention into force (art. VIII). It came into force on 24 August 1962, thirty days after deposit of the sixth such instrument.

percent of the new States and 25 percent of the old States had become parties to the Convention on racial discrimination.

D. TREATIES ON EDUCATIONAL MATTERS AND OBSCENE PUBLICATIONS

This category includes three conventions adopted by the General Conference of UNESCO: (1) Agreement for Facilitating the International Circulation of Visual and Auditory Materials of an Educational, Scientific and Cultural Character, 1949; (2) Agreement on the Importation of Educational, Scientific and Cultural Matters, 1950; (3) International Convention for the Protection of Performers, Producers of Phonograms and Broadcasting Organizations, 1961. It also includes two treaties going back before the United Nations era: (1) Convention for the Suppression of the Circulation of, and Traffic in, Obscene Publications, 1923, as amended by the 1947 Protocol; and (2) Agreement for the Suppression of the Circulation of Obscene Publications, 1910, as amended by the 1949 Protocol.

The two treaties on obscene publications, as amended, have received 47 acceptances each, and the three UNESCO conventions, 23, 57, and 10, respectively. The comparatively high acceptance record of the treaties on obscene publications and of the UNESCO Agreement on the Importation of Educational Materials is partly due to successions by the new States. For example, this UNESCO Convention is in force for 46 percent of the new States and only 40 percent of the old States.

E. TREATIES ON TRANSPORT AND COMMUNICATIONS

The two principal instruments in this group—the Convention on Road Traffic, 1949, and the Convention Concerning Customs Facilities for Touring, 1954—have been accepted by 79 and 61 States, respectively, including 15 and 9 successions by new States. The Protocol on Road Signs and Signals, adopted together with the Convention on Road Traffic, has received only 35 acceptances. This is less than half of the acceptances of the Convention, to which about 47 percent of the new and 79 percent of the old States have become parties.

F. TREATIES ON NARCOTIC DRUGS

Taken together, treaties on narcotic drugs have the highest acceptance record of all groups of treaties: 47 percent of the maximum obtainable. The convention to receive the largest number of acceptances (85 States) of any of the 55 treaties here discussed belongs to this group.[23] This Convention has also received a record number of succes-

---

[23] Convention for Limiting the Manufacture and Regulating the Distribution of Narcotic Drugs, 1931, as amended by the 1946 Protocol.

sions—20. Another treaty in this group has received 80 acceptances;[24] and the latest, the Single Convention on Narcotic Drugs, 1961, has received 66, which is more than any other humanitarian or social treaty was to obtain in the same span of time. Besides, the gap between the proportion of new and old States that have become parties to it (46 and 53 percent) is not, as in the case of other treaties, very large.

It may be noted that the narcotic drugs problem has been a matter of international concern and regulation since at least the turn of this century.[25] Some of the treaties in this group contain simplified procedures of acceptance, which will be reviewed later,[26] and include certain flexible standards of regulations which enable States faced with special situations to adhere to these treaties.

G. Convention on the Recognition and Enforcement of Foreign Arbitral Awards, 1958

By the end of 1968, 34 countries (or 26 percent of the maximum obtainable) had become parties to, and 9 States had signed but not yet ratified, this general treaty, which deals with arbitral awards in the field of private law. The proportion of acceptances by new and old States is 18 percent to 31 percent.

In comparison, the European Convention on International Commercial Arbitration, 1961, has fared much better: 12 of the 31 members (and one non-member) of the E.C.E., or 37 percent, have become parties to it.

IV. THE TEMPO OF ACCEPTANCE

In the following, an analysis is made of the "tempo" (rate of progress) of acceptance of a representative sample of treaties, with a view to discerning patterns, if any, in the "growth" and "peak" periods, and other features of treaties.

For the purpose of this statistical analysis, six treaties each from three groups of general multilateral treaties have been selected: "codification" treaties, human rights treaties, and a mixed category of treaties ranging from the International Convention on Economic Statistics to the Convention on the Enforcement of Foreign Arbitral Awards. Their annual rates of progress of acceptance are recorded in three tables (Symbol A connotes acceptance):

[24] Protocol Bringing under International Control Drugs outside the Scope of the Convention of 1931 for Limiting the Manufacture and Regulating the Distribution of Narcotic Drugs, as amended in 1946.

[25] For an historical perspective on narcotics treaties, see Charles Bevans, "International conventions in the field of narcotic drugs," *Temple Law Quarterly*, vol. 31 (1961), pp. 41-56.

[26] See chap. six.

TABLE I

Tempo of Acceptance of "Codification" Treaties

No.	Name of Treaty, with Date of Adoption	Acceptances											Total A's
		1958	1959	1960	1961	1962	1963	1964	1965	1966	1976	1968	
1	Territorial Sea, 29 April 1958	0	0	5	10	3	3	3	3	6	0	3	36
2	High Seas, 29 April 1958	0	1	5	12	6	3	4	4	5	0	3	43
3	Fishing of the Living Resources of the High Seas, 29 April 1958	0	0	4	3	2	5	3	3	5	0	2	27
4	Continental Shelf, 29 April 1958	0	0	4	9	4	4	3	5	7	0	2	39
5	Diplomatic Relations, 18 April 1961	—	—	—	0	9	11	15	19	3	8	17	82
6	Consular Relations, 24 April 1963	—	—	—	—	—	1	4	12	4	6	6	33

TABLE II
Tempo of Acceptance of Some Human Rights Treaties

No.	Name of Treaty, with Date of Adoption	Acceptances																					Total A's
		48	49	50	51	52	53	54	55	56	57	58	59	60	61	62	63	64	65	66	67	68	
1	Genocide, 9 Dec. 1948	0	5	23	3	9	3	5	2	5	1	3	4	2	0	1	1	0	1	1	2	2	73
2	Suppression of Traffic, 21 Mar. 1950	—	—	1	2	5	2	2	4	3	1	5	2	1	0	4	1	1	2	1	0	2	39
3	Refugees, 28 July 1951	—	—	—	0	1	4	8	4	4	2	0	1	4	5	5	5	4	2	2	2	1	54
4	Pol. Rts. of Women, 20 Dec. 1952	—	—	—	—	0	3	15	4	2	4	3	2	1	2	3	2	3	2	5	4	6	61
5	Suppl. Conv. on Slavery, 30 Apr. 1956	—	—	—	—	—	—	—	—	0	11	14	8	3	2	6	10	7	2	5	4	1	73
6	Racial Discrimination, 21 Dec. 1965	—	—	—	—	—	—	—	—	—	—	—	—	—	—	—	—	—	—	5	13	9	27

TABLE III
Tempo of Acceptance of Some Other Treaties

No.	Name of Treaty, with Date of Adoption	Acceptances																					Total A's
		48	49	50	51	52	53	54	55	56	57	58	59	60	61	62	63	64	65	66	67	68	
1	Econ. Stat., 1928, Amended 9 Dec. 1948	6	7	3	0	4	1	0	0	0	0	1	0	0	0	0	0	0	1				23
2	Road Traffic, 19 Sept. 1949	—	0	3	1	8	3	2	3	5	8	6	3	3	5	16	4	3	4	1	1	0	79
3	Importation of Educational Materials, 17 June 1950	—	—	0	3	10	2	2	2	1	5	4	2	2	1	6	4	2	3	3	1	4	57
4	Customs Facilities, 4 June 1954	—	—	—	—	—	—	0	6	6	7	10	5	3	3	5	6	2	1	3	3	1	61
5	Single Conv. on Narcotic Drugs, 30 Mar. 1961	—	—	—	—	—	—	—	—	—	—	—	—	—	3	10	10	20	8	3	8	4	66
6	Foreign Arbitral Awards, 10 June 1958	—	—	—	—	—	—	—	—	—	—	0	7	5	7	7	0	3	1	1	2	1	34

SOME INFERENCES REGARDING THE TEMPO

Table I indicates that for the four law of the sea treaties, there were no acceptances during the remainder of the year in which they were adopted. During the next calendar year, there was only one acceptance; the normal growth period lasted until the ninth calendar year; interest in the subject matter of the treaties revived in the eleventh calendar year; and for three of these four treaties, the peak was during the fourth calendar year (1961), by which time the number of eligible parties had also increased.

The Convention on Diplomatic Relations, 1961, which has the highest record of all "codification" treaties, exhibits somewhat different features. Its annual rate of progress of acceptance has been faster than that of any law of the sea treaty. It reached its peak during the fourth calendar year following the year of adoption, almost like the Conventions on the law of the sea, but its peak (19 acceptances within 1965) was much higher than that of the latter. Also noteworthy is the second peak for the Convention on Diplomatic Relations (17 acceptances) during 1968. Interest in this Convention evidently revived in 1968, after the General Assembly appealed through resolution 2328 (XXII) to all eligible States to ratify or accede to it among other international instruments.[27] The Convention on Consular Relations, 1963, has made relatively slower progress than the Convention on Diplomatic Relations. But its peak (12 acceptances) occurred in the second calendar year after the year of adoption (1965, the same year in which the 1961 Convention on Diplomatic Relations reached its peak of 19 acceptances). It appears to be still in its growth period, like the Convention on Diplomatic Relations; but it was unable to engender, as a result of the General Assembly resolution just mentioned, a comparable interest.

Table II indicates that the initial tempo of acceptances of human rights treaties has usually been faster than that of codification treaties[28] (see table I). In fact, for three of the six human rights treaties, the peak (and for a fourth, the first peak) was reached during the second calendar year following the year of adoption and hence also, on the whole, earlier

[27] See chap. three.

[28] To what extent this has accelerated the entering into force of human rights treaties depended, of course, on two factors: the required number of ratifications or accesions, and the perio dof time between the date of deposit of the last such instrument and the date of entry into force. For example, the Genocide Convention required twenty such instruments, which were deposited by 14 October 1950, less than two years after its adoption on 9 December 1948. It came into effect on 12 January 1951, the 90th day following the date of the deposit of the 20th instrument (art. XIII, para. 2). The Supplementary Convention on Slavery, adopted on 30 April 1956, entered into force exactly one year later on 30 April 1957, the day on which the second State had become a party to it (art. 13, para. 1).

than for the codification treaties. On the other hand, the figures for the human rights treaties[29] show that thereafter the over-all average rate of acceptances has been comparatively slower than that of the codification treaties.

Since these human rights treaties, with one exception, were adopted earlier than the codification treaties, the figures for the former also show the growth rate of acceptances during the second decade following their adoption. As seen on table II, there was a gradual decline in the tempo of acceptances during the second decade, but the trend was different for one of them: 22 countries became parties to the Convention on the Political Rights of Women during the first six years of the second decade, as against only 16 during the last six years of the first decade.

As in the case of codification treaties, United Nations promotional efforts appear to have contributed also to the relatively higher rate of acceptances of certain human rights treaties in certain years.[30]

Table III, covering treaties on different subjects, exhibits a variety in tempo, or growth rate of acceptances. The record of the 1928 Convention on Economic Statistics, as amended in 1948, differs from that of all treaties not only in this group, but in the groups covered by tables I and II. After a relatively good start in the first three years and a revival of interest in the fifth, only three additional countries adhered to it during the subsequent thirteen years. The tempo of acceptances of the Convention on Road Transport, 1949, reached its peak extraordinarily late, in the fourteenth calendar year. Its average rate of acceptances during its exceptionally long growth period was comparatively higher than that of other treaties. The Agreement on Importation of Educational Materials, 1950, like many other treaties, reached its peak during the second calendar year after its creation. Although after 18 years this Agreement, with 57 States parties to it, still does not range within the highest level, it has received acceptances steadily every year and thus retained its momentum. The Single Convention on Narcotic Drugs, 1961, which progressed relatively faster than many others, attained its peak during the third calendar year after adoption, and within eight years, more States (66) had adhered to it than, for example, to any of the law of the sea Conventions after ten years (36, 43, 27 and 39, respectively; see table I) or to the Convention on the Political Rights of Women after sixteen years (61; see table II). The Convention on Customs Facilities, 1954, after reaching its peak in the fourth calendar year following adoption,

---

[29] Evidently, no indication in this respect exists as yet with respect to the Convention on Racial Discrimination, which, by the end of 1968, had been open for acceptance only three years.

[30] See chap. three.

maintained a fairly constant growth of acceptances during the next five years and a somewhat lower growth rate during the subsequent half decade. The Convention on Foreign Arbitral Awards showed an almost even and relatively high growth rate during each of the first four years following the year of adoption, but decline in acceptances started immediately thereafter: during the past six years, fewer countries (six altogether) became parties to it than during each but one for the first four years.

CHAPTER THREE

INTERNATIONAL MEASURES TO FOSTER ACCEPTANCES

Treaties adopted by organs of international organizations, or under their auspices, are useful to the extent to which they are applied; hence the concern and efforts of international organizations that they be widely adhered to. This concern is clearly implied in certain provisions of some of the treaties themselves. As also indicated by the survey that follows, international organizations have used a considerable variety of other methods to foster interest in and adherence to such treaties.

I. PROMOTION OF ACCEPTANCES OF TREATIES

A. APPEALS BY THE GENERAL ASSEMBLY AND ECOSOC

One method for international agencies to promote wider acceptance of international instruments is through appeals addressed to all Member States, to certain categories of Member States or to other eligible States. Such appeals are regularly couched in general terms and thus do not contain the detailed factual and legal information of interest to government lawyers. While formally addressed to Governments, they are designed to awaken or strengthen interest in the respective treaties not only on the part of Governments but also of legislators concerned and of groups and individuals who could be instrumental in making States adhere to the treaty in question. They are therefore aimed also at fostering the interest of public opinion and soliciting support from non-governmental organizations.[1]

---

[1] Some resolutions urging wider acceptance of human rights treaties seem to have been stimulated, *inter alia,* by promotional activities of non-governmental organizations. Regarding the role of such organizations in general, see sec. E below.

If States not yet parties to a treaty vote in favour of such an appeal, they include themselves among the States addressed by the appeal. (Not infrequently, such appeals are adopted by unanimous vote.) Interestingly, the question of whether a positive vote for the resolution creates an expectation, on the principle of good faith, that thereupon the respective Governments will give serious consideration to obtaining the treaty's ratification, seems not to have been raised in the United Nations or in the legal literature.

1. *Resolutions by the General Assembly*

The General Assembly has frequently urged States to adhere to treaties, especially treaties adopted under United Nations auspices, but occasionally others as well. Such urging may accompany or closely follow the adoption of a treaty, or it may refer to a treaty or treaties previously adopted.

For example, on 16 December 1966, when after long efforts the Assembly adopted the two international Covenants on Human Rights and the related Optional Protocol, it expressed its "hope" that they "will be signed and ratified or acceded to without delay," and indicated the Assembly's intention to consider the status of ratification at its future sessions.[2]

At its 22nd and 23rd sessions alone, the General Assembly urged adherence to numerous instruments; namely, the Conventions on Privileges and Immunities of the United Nations, 1946, and on Diplomatic Relations, 1961;[3] the Agreement on the Rescue of Astronauts;[4] the Treaty for the Prohibition of Nuclear Weapons in Latin America;[5] the

---

[2] The intention is shown in operative para. 3 of the res. 2200 (XXI) request(ing) the Secretary-General to submit to the General Assembly at its future sessions reports concerning the state of ratifications of the Covenants and of the Optional Protocol which will be considered by the Assembly as a separate agenda item.
Regarding subsequent res. 2337 (XXII) of 18 December 1967, see note 6, below.

[3] "The General Assembly . . . urges States Members of the United Nations which have not yet done so to accede" to the 1946 Convention, and "States which have not yet done so to ratify or accede to" the 1961 Convention (res. 2328 (XXII)).

[4] "The General Assembly . . . 1. Commends the Agreement . . . ; 2. Requests the Depositary Governments to open [it] for signature and ratification at the earliest possible date; 3. Expresses its hope for the widest possible adherence" to it (res. 2345 (XXII)).
In res. 2453B (XXIII), the Assembly, "Welcoming the entry into force" of the Agreement, "Urges" non-parties "to give early consideration" to accepting it.

[5] "The General Assembly . . . Noting that it is the intent of the signatory States that all existing States within the zone defined in the Treaty may become parties . . . 3. Recommends States . . . to strive to take all the measures within their power to ensure that the Treaty speedily obtains the

two International Covenants on Human Rights, 1966, and the related Optional Protocol;[6] the Treaty on Non-Proliferation of Nuclear Weapons;[7] the Outer Space Treaty;[8] the Partial Test Ban Treaty, 1963;[9] the 1967 Agreement concerning "International Monetary Reform";[10] several international instruments concerning "human rights in armed conflict";[11] and United Nations, I.L.O. and UNESCO instruments against Racial Discrimination.

The last-mentioned resolution[12] referring to the instruments against racial discrimination is particularly elaborate. In it, the Assembly

---

widest possible application among them; 4. Invites Powers possessing nuclear weapons to sign and ratify Additional Protocol II of the Treaty as soon as possible." (Res. 2286 (XXII).)

In res. 2456B (XXIII) the Assembly "reiterates . . . the urgent appeal" of the Conference of Non-Nuclear Weapon States "for full compliance by the nuclear-weapon Powers with para. 4" of the resolution just mentioned, "in which the Assembly invited" them "to sign and ratify Additional Protocol II of the Treaty as soon as possible."

[6] "The General Assembly . . . Desiring to accelerate the ratification and accessions to the Covenants and the Protocol, Convinced that the Principles and Purposes of the Charter of the United Nations would be greatly enhanced by [their] coming into force, 1. Invites States which are eligible to become Parties to [them] to hasten their ratifications or accessions . . ." (Res. 2337(XXII)).

[7] See text of this study.

[8] The General Assembly "urges" countries not yet parties "to give early considerations" to accepting it.

[9] "The General Assembly . . . Noting with regret that all States have not yet adhered to the Treaty . . . 1. Urges all States which have not done so to adhere without further delay to the Treaty . . ." (res. 2455 XXIII)).

[10] "The General Assembly . . . Calls upon the Governments of the States members of the International Monetary Fund to take the necessary steps for the early ratification and activation of the Special Drawing Rights facility," agreed upon in 1967 by the IMF Board of Governors, "which is intended to improve the functioning of the world economy . . ." (res. 2461 (XXIII)).

[11] "The General Assembly . . . Calls upon all States which have not yet done so to become parties to the Hague Conventions of 1899 and 1907, the Geneva Protocol [for the Prohibition of the Use in War of Asphyxiating, Poisonous or Other Gases, and of Bacteriological Methods of Warfare] of 1925, and the Geneva [Red Cross] Conventions of 1949" (res. 2444 (XXIII) of 19 December 1968, titled "Respect for Human Rights in Armed Conflicts," adopted unanimously). Regarding in particular the Geneva Protocol of 1925, the Assembly in another resolution (2454A (XXIII), adopted one day later by a vote of 107 to 0, with 2 abstentions) "reiterates its call [issued in res. 2162B (XXI) of 5 December 1966] for strict observance by all States of the principles and objectives of the Geneva Protocol of 17 June 1925 and invites all States to accede to that Protocol."

[12] Resolution 2332 (XXII) on "Measures for the Speedy Implementation of International Instruments against Racial Discrimination," adopted on 18 December 1967 by a vote of 106 to 2, with 2 abstentions.

(a) "urges all eligible Governments which have not yet done so to sign, ratify and implement without delay the International Convention on . . . Racial Discrimination and the other Conventions directed against discrimination in employment and occupation [International Labour Convention No. 111, of 1958] and against discrimination in education [UNESCO Convention, 1960]";

(b) "requests the Secretary-General to make available to the Commission on Human Rights . . . the information submitted by Governments of Member States on measures taken for the speedy implementation of the United Nations Declaration on the Elimination of All Forms of Racial Discrimination";

(c) requests propagation of the Convention and the Declaration on the widest scale, by requesting "the Secretary-General, the specialized agencies and all organizations concerned to continue to take measures to propagate, through appropriate channels, the principles and norms set forth" in the two instruments; and

(d) "recommends that the Commission on Human Rights continue to give consideration . . . to measures for the speedy implementation of the Declaration. . ."

Mention should be made of the resolution regarding the Treaty on the Non-Proliferation of Nuclear Weapons (2373 (XXII) of 12 June 1968) because it resulted from an intensive debate in the General Assembly on the very question of whether or not the Assembly should commend the Treaty to Member States for adherence.[13] The resumed 22nd session of the Assembly decided in the affirmative. The resolution "commends the Treaty" and, in fact,

> expresses the hope for the widest possible adherence to the Treaty by both nuclear-weapon and non-nuclear-weapon States (paras. 1 and 3).

Furthermore, the resolution endeavours to dispel concerns that may dissuade Governments from adhering to the Treaty, first by taking the unusual step of giving an interpretation of the Treaty:

> The Assembly (is) convinced that, pursuant to the provisions of the Treaty, all signatories have the right to engage in research, production and use of nuclear energy for peaceful purposes and will be able to acquire source and special fissionable materials, as well as equipment for the processing, use and production of nuclear material for peaceful purposes (Preamble, para. 4);

---

[13] As regards the issue of the non-proliferation of nuclear weapons, the Assembly began in 1960 to appeal to all Governments to achieve an agreement (res. 1576 (XV) of 20 December 1960 and 1665 (XVI) of 4 December 1961). By 1965, the Assembly provided guidelines to the Eighteen-Nation Disarmament Committee for the negotiations of such a treaty (res. 2028 (XX) of 19 November 1965), and in res. 2346 (XXII) of 19 December 1967, it reaffirmed that further efforts to conclude such a treaty were "imperative."

and secondly, by expressing the Assembly's "conviction" that the Treaty "will contribute" to the taking of "effective measures on the cessation of the nuclear arms race and on nuclear disarmament," which measures must follow as soon as possible (rather than precede) an agreement to prevent the further proliferation of nuclear weapons (Preamble, para. 5).

2. *Resolutions by ECOSOC*

The ECOSOC has also variously issued appeals and recommendations to States to accept treaties on subjects within its concern, for example, regarding the Convention on the Political Rights of Women, 1953,[14] and anti-slavery treaties.[15]

Since States, when adhering to international conventions, do not refer to Assembly or ECOSOC resolutions of this kind, their impact is difficult to gauge. However, periodic resolutions promoting some treaties seem to have fostered acceptances.

B. CONCENTRATED CAMPAIGNS

Between 1959-1968 the United Nations designated three twelve-month periods during which international attention would focus on matters of major concern: (1) the world refugee problem, (2) the need for closer international co-operation and (3) the promotion of human rights. All three of these extensive programmes, carried out in co-ordination with inter-governmental, governmental and non-governmental organizations, constituted promotional campaigns aiming at wider acceptance of specified United Nations conventions.

1. *World Refugee Year (1 July 1959-30 June 1960)*

In resolution 1285 (XIII) of 5 December 1958, the Assembly urged all Members of the United Nations or any specialized agency "to co-operate . . . from a humanitarian point of view, in promoting a World Refugee Year as a practical means of securing increased assistance for refugees throughout the world."[16] The assistance was to take the form of creating opportunities for voluntary repatriation, resettlement or integration of refugees (thereby changing their status to non-refugees); of collecting voluntary funds for the work of the United Nations High Commissioner for Refugees; of increasing the activities of voluntary agencies on behalf of refugees; and of issuing additional refugee visas by Governments. Additional acceptances of the Refugee Convention of 1951

[14] See ECOSOC res. 504E (XVI), 547B (XVIII), 652B (XXIV) and 1068B (XXXIX).
[15] See ECOSOC res. 772D (XXX), 826E (XXXII), 890 (XXXIV), 1077 (XXXIX) and 1126 (XLI).
[16] Since the end of the Second World War, an estimated 40 million people have become refugees; perhaps 15 million were still in that status in 1959 when the "Year" was organized.

were also urged. In this respect, the campaign was less successful than in others.[17]

2. *International Co-operation Year (1965)*

The United Nations Preparatory Committee suggested that the Secretary-General appeal to Member States to give consideration to the early ratification of the multilateral treaties for which he acts as depositary. By a letter dated 2 March 1964 and addressed to the Permanent Representatives of Members, the Secretary-General did so, referring to eleven conventions in five fields: diplomatic and consular relations, law of the sea, human rights, privileges and immunities, educational and cultural co-operation.[18]

During the Year, sixteen States replied that they were giving earnest consideration to the early ratification of some or all of the specified treaties.[19] Notwithstanding the relatively small number of non-committal answers, the acceptance record of most of these instruments improved between 1965 and 1967,[20] and informal interviews with officials of the foreign offices of some States have indicated that the Year gave an impetus to considerations of acceptance during 1965 and thereafter.

3. *International Human Rights Year (1968)*

The experience of the International Co-operation Year (1965) suggested that by the end of 1968 it was too early to gauge the impact of the Human Rights Year. Just before the close of the latter (31 December 1968), the first country (Costa Rica) ratified the two International Covenants on Human Rights of December 1966; and on 4 January 1969, the Convention on Racial Discrimination entered into force, the 27th country (Poland) having deposited its ratification on 5 December 1968.[21]

---

[17] During 1959 there was only one new adherence and during 1960 four adherences, to the Refugee Convention. But this may have been due to the fact that the Convention focuses on persons who became refugees prior to 1 January 1951. Regarding the Refugee Protocol concerning persons who became refugees thereafter, see below.

[18] A/AC.118/L.2. The letter listed the following treaties: the Vienna Conventions on Diplomatic Relations, 1961, and Consular Relations, 1963; the four Conventions on the law of the sea, 1958; the Supplementary Slavery Convention, 1956; the Genocide Convention, 1948; the Convention on the Privileges and Immunities of the United Nations; the Convention on the Privileges and Immunities of the Specialised Agencies, 1947; the Agreement on the Importation of Educational and Cultural Materials, 1950.

[19] See the Report of the Committee for the International Co-operation Year, U.N. Doc. A/5836, p. 3.

[20] For example, additional acceptances made the Vienna Convention on Consular Relations, 1963, enter into force on 19 March 1967.

[21] The other 26 States that had ratified the Convention are: Argentina, Brazil, Bulgaria, Costa Rica, Cyprus, Czechoslovakia, Ecuador, Ghana, Hungary, Iceland, India, Iran, Kuwait, Niger, Nigeria, Pakistan, Panama,

As mentioned before,[22] the International Conference on Human Rights variously urged adherence to instruments relating to human rights and called upon the General Assembly "to take steps in order to ensure . . . the widest possible accession to them."[23]

C. PROMOTIONAL ACTIVITIES BY THE SECRETARY-GENERAL AND SUBSIDIARY BODIES

The United Nations has also made use of somewhat more formal methods than those just described to promote wider acceptance of treaties.

1. *Inquiries by the Secretary-General*

Even before the start of the International Year for Human Rights, the General Assembly at its 23rd session showed concern about "the small number of signatures" received by the two comprehensive International Conventions on Human Rights which it had adopted at its preceding session. In resolution 2337 (XXII) of 18 December 1967 (adopted by a vote of 112 to 0, with no abstentions), the Assembly used the device of requesting the Secretary-General to report on the status of these instruments and the related Optional Protocol to the Teheran International Conference on Human Rights, and to the 23rd session of the Assembly. The note verbale thereupon addressed by the Secretary-General to the Governments of all eligible States requested them "to provide any indication which they might wish to transmit" regarding ratification of or accession to the three instruments. From the replies of the 23 Governments received as of 10 October 1968, it appears that in most of these countries, the instruments were being examined by competent authorities with a view to their acceptance.[24]

2. *Action by the Secretary-General regarding certain treaties concluded under League of Nations auspices*

General Assembly resolution 1903 (XVIII) of 18 November 1963[25] noted that "many" new States were unable to accede to twenty-

---

the Philippines, Poland, Sierra Leone, Spain, Tunisia, the United Arab Republic, Uruguay, Venezuela, Yugoslavia.

[22] See chap. one of this study.

[23] *Ibid.*

[24] See U.N. Doc. A/7276. (Regarding the Secretary-General's inquiry about adherence to the Convention on the Recognition and Enforcement of Foreign Arbitral Awards, 1958, see below.)

[25] For its deliberation on this item, the Assembly had at its disposal a report of the International Law Commission. See *Official Records of the General Assembly, 18th session, Supplement No. 9* (A/5509), paras. 18-50. Regarding the debate in the Sixth Committee preceding adoption of res. 1903 (XVIII), see *Official Records of the General Assembly, 18th session, 6th Committee,* 795th to 802nd meetings.

one general multilateral treaties of technical and non-political character concluded under League of Nations auspices, "for lack of an invitation to accede" (the Council of the League, authorized to extend such invitations, having ceased to exist). The resolution requested the Secretary-General (a) to "consult, where necessary," with specified States "as to whether any of the treaties in question have ceased to be in force, have been superseded by later treaties, have otherwise ceased to be of interest for accession by additional States, or require action to adapt them to contemporary conditions," and (b) to invite "each" eligible State, not only newly independent States, to become parties to the treaties in question.

Pursuant to this mandate, the Secretary-General requested fifty-four States parties to any of these treaties to advise him of their opinions regarding the questions just mentioned on those treaties. However, since sufficient evidence existed that two of the twenty-one instruments (Convention for the Suppression of Counterfeiting Currency and Protocol thereto, both of 1929) were fully operative, he invited States not yet parties to accede to them.

On the basis of the replies received,[26] the General Assembly "recognise(d)" that in addition to the two instruments relating to counterfeiting, nine specified treaties "may be of interest for accession by additional States."[27]

3. *United Nations Commission on International Trade Law (UNCITRAL)*

This Commission was established by the unanimously adopted General Assembly resolution 2205 (XXI) of 17 December 1966. Consisting of twenty-nine States elected by the Assembly for six-year terms, UNCITRAL aims to further the progressive harmonization and unification of the law of international trade by, *inter alia,* "promoting

---

[26] The Secretary-General's report to the Assembly of 25 February 1965 observed that "the replies were not numerous; in respect to most of the treaties fewer than one third of the parties consulted answered. . . ." Some additional replies were received after the Secretary-General had in a second note advised States that the question was included in the provisional agenda of the 20th session of the Assembly. (See *Official Records of the General Assembly, 20th sessison, Annexes,* agenda item 88, Doc. A/5759 and Add.1.)

[27] Resolution 2021 (XX) of 5 November 1965. The resolution also "draws the attention of the parties to the desirability of adapting some of these treaties to contemporary conditions, particularly in the event that new parties should so request."

Regarding the debates in the Sixth Committee preceding the adoption of the resolution, see *Official Records of the General Assembly, 20th session, 6th Committee,* 853rd to 857th meetings. See, for example, one representative's statement that res. 1903 (XVIII) had enabled his country to accede to the two instruments relating to counterfeiting. (*Ibid.,* 857th meeting para 25.)

wider participation in existing international conventions," "preparing or promoting the adoption of new international conventions" and "promoting ways and means of ensuring a uniform interpretation and application of international conventions."

At its first regular session, held in early 1968, UNCITRAL decided to give priority to, among other topics, the harmonization and unification of the law of international commercial arbitration. In this connexion, it decided to draw the attention of Member States of the United Nations to the existence of the Convention on the Recognition and Enforcement of Foreign Arbitral Awards, 1958, and to invite them to consider the possibility of adhering to it.[28]

Pursuant to this decision, the Secretary-General brought the Convention to the attention of Members, asking those not parties to indicate by 31 December 1968 whether they intended to adhere to it.

D. REGIONAL INTER-GOVERNMENTAL ORGANIZATIONS

The Assembly of Heads of State and Government of the Organization of African Unity (Kinshasa, September 1967) recommended to all member States of the O.A.U. to accede to the Refugee Convention, 1951, and the Refugee Protocol, 1967. Shortly thereafter, the Conference on the Legal, Economic and Social Aspects of African Refugee Problems (Addis Ababa, October 1967), attended by the most senior officials responsible for refugee work from 22 African countries, drew the attention of African Governments, the United Nations and world opinion to the serious refugee problem in Africa. The Conference declared itself "convinced that it is a matter of urgency for all African countries which have not already done so to accede to" these two instruments.[29] The Inter-American Commission on Human Rights of the Organization of American States similarly recommended adherence to them by members of the O.A.S.[30]

One agenda item of the 9th session of the European Committee on Legal Cooperation was the consideration of the "number of ratifications of universal conventions by Member States" of the Council of Europe.[31]

In this connexion, reference may also be made to the following devices to promote acceptance of inter-American treaties and conventions

[28] *Official Records of the General Assembly, 23rd session, Supplement No. 16* (A/7216), p. 24.

[29] Conference on the Legal, Economic and Social Aspects of African Refugee Problems, Addis Ababa, 9-18 October 1967, p. 2.

[30] See O.A.S. official records, OEA/Ser.L/V/11.18, Doc. 23 (English), 30 October 1967.

[31] Statement by the Director of Legal Affairs, Council of Europe, at the 985th meeting of the International Law Commission. (Report of the I.L.C. on the work of its 20th session, *Official Records of the General Assembly, 23rd session, Supplement No. 9*) (A/7209/Rev. 1), p. 33.

recommended by the 8th International Conference of American States, Lima, 1938. The Conference requested the Pan American Union to continue publication of charts showing the status of those instruments and authorized the Director General when sending them to member Governments "to inquire regarding the status of the agreements and the progress that is being made toward their ratification." The Conference also supported the proposal of the preceding Conference (Montevideo, 1933) to designate in each member State "a Representative *ad honorem* of the Pan American Union whose duty would be to expedite the study, approval and ratification of Inter-American treaties and conventions."[32]

E. NON-GOVERNMENTAL ORGANIZATIONS

It has long been evident that non-governmental organizations have played a significant part in the promotion of multilateral treaties, particularly in the humanitarian and social fields. The human rights provisions of the United Nations Charter, the I.L.O. Convention on the Abolition of Forced Labour and the Supplementary Convention on Slavery are well-known examples of their contributions. In some cases, non-governmental organizations have influenced the attitudes of Governments and legislators towards the acceptance of particular treaties. For example, the Anti-Slavery Society has successfully advocated the ratification of slavery conventions. Religious and trade union organizations have been active in promoting the conventions on the elimination of discrimination, as have automobile associations and travel organizations in promoting the acceptance of treaties on transport and customs. More recently, international associations of lawyers and judges have been actively concerned with the promotion of multilateral treaties.

F. PROMOTION BY THE INTER-PARLIAMENTARY UNION (IPU)

The Inter-Parliamentary Union—an international organization of legislatures[33]—has long been active in promoting international law and treaties. The annual Conferences of the IPU have from time to time adopted resolutions urging legislators to campaign for their Governments' adherence to specified treaties. Such resolutions referred to the Convention on the Political Rights of Women, the Refugee Convention, UNESCO conventions in the field of education and others.

Other IPU resolutions have advocated certain policies bearing on problems connected with the acceptance of international instruments. Two such resolutions adopted by the Forty-second Annual Inter-Parliamentary Conference are of special relevance:

---

[32] Pan-American Union, *Handbook, Fourth meeting of the Inter-American Council of Jurists, Santiago de Chile, 24 August 1959* (Washington, D.C.), pp. 19-20.

[33] At present there are sixty-five national groups comprising members of legislature in the Inter-Parliamentary Union.

Governments should so far as practicable keep Parliaments informed of the main course of international negotiations, so that Parliaments may be enabled to express their views upon such negotiation; delegations in charge of such negotiations should, as far as possible, include Members of Parliament.

Governments which have signed international conventions' agreements should, whenever appropriate, submit them to their respective Parliaments as soon as possible for ratification or acceptance.[34]

The first recommendation manifests the concern of the Inter-Parliamentary Union to increase the role of members of legislatures in the negotiation of treaties. The usefulness of including prominent legislators in the negotiation of treaties has been indicated by the informal discussions held with legal officials of States that have comparatively high records of acceptance of treaties. The officials attributed such records to the policy of their Governments of including members of legislatures in the negotiation of treaties.

The second recommendation is also significant, as it expresses the concern of the organization of parliamentarians that treaties be submitted by the executive for legislative approval without delay.

In a symposium on "Present Day Problems of Parliament" held in 1965 under the auspices of the IPU, some other useful ideas were expressed on the role and functions of legislatures in the negotiation and conclusion of multilateral treaties; for example, that the Foreign Affairs Committee should be associated with the elaboration of the Government's main negotiating positions and kept informed of the most important developments in the diplomatic field.[35]

Apart from its formal deliberations, the Inter-Parliamentary Union provides possibilities for informal consultations among legislators the world over. This facilitates the exchange of information in various States about developments in legislative approval of treaties.

II. REPORTING BY STATES TO INTERNATIONAL ORGANIZATIONS

"The rendering of reports to an international authority is a procedure of long standing, used even before the establishment of the United Nations."[36] Members of international organizations may be re-

[34] Inter-Parliamentary Union (Geneva), *Resolutions adopted by Inter-Parliamentary Conferences and Principal Decisions of the Council* (1953-1960), pp. 19-20.

[35] See *Inter-Parliamentary Union Bulletin* (First Quarter No. 1, 1966), p. 65.

[36] United Nations, *Methods used by the United Nations in the Field of Human Rights.* A/Conf. 32/6 (1968), especially pp. 124-134, citing art. 22 of the Covenant of the League of Nations, art. 19 and 22 of the I.L.O. Constitution, Art. 87(a), 88, 83, 73(e) of the Charter of the United Nations and art. VIII of the UNESCO Constitution.

quested to report on various subjects and for various purposes, including the purpose of enabling international organs to examine the behaviour of States with regard to adherence to treaties. Experience has validated the assumption that such examination can result in an increase in acceptances.

In its simplest form, the reporting approach does not impose upon Governments a specific obligation: one international organ merely reports, on the basis of information in its possession, to another international organ about actions and attitudes of Governments. Under another form, the Governments themselves assume the obligation to report to the international body concerned. The Government's involvement then increases if the procedure becomes more strict; that is, if they have to transmit more detailed information either to the organ making or to the organ receiving the report, or to both. Sometimes Governments are also expected to observe time limits for the consideration of acceptance.[37]

Thus the reporting approach contains, depending upon specific arrangements, varying degrees of inquiry, although never of control of Governments' actions and attitudes. Their sovereign discretion regarding acceptance or non-acceptance is not questioned: if they are asked to report thereon and explain the facts reported, they are merely to be induced to exercise this discretion.

A. LEAGUE OF NATIONS

As the number of multilateral conventions adopted under League auspices gradually increased during its first half decade, the Assembly became concerned about lagging acceptance of some of them. By 1926, it invited the Council of the League

> to call for a report every six months on the progress of ratification [of international agreements and conventions concluded under the League's auspices] and to consider methods for securing the more rapid bringing into force of these agreements and conventions.[38]

Thereupon the Council, as its first step, requested the Secretary-General of the League to submit to its next session a report on the progress made in regard to the ratification of those international treaties.[39]

---

[37] It may be noted that if an international organ wishes to deliberate about, or in any other manner use, information regarding the acceptance records of States, it is in the interest of States to furnish such information themselves.

[38] See League of Nations, resolution adopted by the Assembly on 23 September 1926 (A.98.1926.V).

[39] The Secretary-General's report listed in chronological order the multilateral instruments by then concluded under League auspices; the States which had ratified or acceded to them; the States which had signed but not ratified them; and finally, the States which had neither signed nor acceded, although they had participated in the conference at which the agreements were drawn up or had been invited to become parties thereto (League of Nations, C.32.1927.V).

Thereafter, the question of ratification of League-sponsored conventions appeared frequently on the agenda of the Council. Although these debates necessarily drew upon information from Member Governments, the Council refrained from formally instituting a duty or making requests to furnish such information. It can, however, be surmised that the attention paid by the Council to the matter induced members of the Council to proceed with ratifications.[40] The positive impact can be discerned from the ratification record of Council members. In 1929, Yugoslavia became a member of the Council after nearly a decade of membership in the League, during which time it ratified but one convention. During the next two years, however, it adhered to twenty-five conventions.[41] Similarly, Norway, after being elected to the Council in 1930, ratified twenty-four conventions in the years 1930-1932.[42]

Two plenipotentiary conferences held under League auspices[43] in 1928 and 1929 laid down that signatories of specific agreements who did not ratify within two years after signature should notify the Secretary-General of the League of their position.

A significant step was taken by an Assembly resolution of 24 September 1929 which requested the Council to set up a Committee

> to investigate . . . the reasons for delays which still exist and the means by which the number of signatures, ratifications or accessions given to [these] conventions could be increased.[44]

The Council appointed a Committee of eight members

> in order that all the various views which may help to solve a problem of the greatest importance for the Members of the League may find expression on the Committee.[45]

This phrasing of the Committee's terms of reference is cautious, but the report produced by the Committee showed remarkable vigour and was unanimous.[46]

Several of the measures recommended by the Committee would have relied on the efficacy of reporting. These measures held that:

[40] During the Council's 49th session, M. Briand (France) stated that he would do his utmost to ensure that the League conventions not yet ratified by France would be ratified as soon as possible (League of Nations, *Official Journal,* Apr. 1928, p. 381). Similar instances are to be found in the records of the Council.

[41] Francis Wilcox, *The Ratification of International Conventions* (London, 1935), p. 133.

[42] *Ibid.*

[43] The Conference on Economic Statistics, in art. VI of its Final Act of 14 December 1928, and the Conference for the Adoption of a Convention for the Suppresssion of Counterfeiting Currency, in art. II of the Final Act of 20 April 1929.

[44] Quoted in the Committee's report dated 9 May 1930, No. A.10.1930. V, p. 1.

[45] *Ibid.*

[46] For the text of the Committee's report, see *ibid.*

(1) All signatories should be requested by resolution of the Assembly to state their positions regarding conventions not ratified by them.

(2) Future general conventions concluded under League auspices might usefully incorporate (with appropriate modifications) the rules applicable to I.L.O. conventions.

(3) In particular, every Conference adopting a convention should also establish a time limit, after which any signatory that had not become a party would (a) have to take steps to obtain ratification from its legislature, or (b) if its constitution did not require legislative ratification, report to the League on its intentions.[47] The obligation would apply only to signatories, but regardless of whether a Government signed at the Conference or thereafter.

The Assembly, by resolution of 3 October 1930,[48] adopted a far-reaching recommendation of the Committee. It required the Secretary-General to request Governments whose signature to a League convention remained unratified after one year from the closing of the protocol of signature to inform him about their intentions concerning ratification. The information obtained by the Secretary-General[49] was then submitted to the Assembly for its consideration.

The resolution also stipulated that if States had not signed or acceded to a general League convention within five years after it was opened for signature, the Secretary-General was to inquire from them whether a possibility of their accession existed or whether any objections to the substance of the convention prevented them from accepting it.

The record of acceptances supports the assertion that "the ratification of international Conventions [was] greatly speeded up by the continuous efforts put by the machinery of the League of Nations."[50]

---

[47] "The Government of each State would undertake, within a certain period (to be fixed by the Conference at which the convention is drawn up) from the date of its signature, if parliamentary approval or legislation were necessary in that State before ratification, either to submit the convention to its Parliament for approval together with drafts of any legislation necessary, or to inform the Secretary-General of the League in writing of its intentions with regard to the convention; and that the Government of each State, in which parliamentary action is not necessary before ratification, would undertake to inform the Secretary-General of the League of its intentions with regard to the convention, in the event of its not having deposited its ratification within the fixed period." *Ibid.*, p. 5.

[48] Text in *L.o.N. Records of the 11th Ordinary Session of the Assembly, Plenary meetings,* pp. 215-217, which is reproduced in annex VI of this study.

[49] Wilcox, *op. cit.*, p. 147, notes that the Secretary-General's requests for this information on the whole met with success.

[50] Wilcox, *op. cit.*, p. 155, citing various ratification figures. For example, the Opium Convention of 1912 never came into force, but the Convention of 1925 on the same subject was, as of September 1934, ratified by 49 Members and non-members of the League. Similarly, whereas only 9

B. United Nations

The United Nations has generally not used practices similar to those of the League of Nations just described. However, two United Nations organs have applied the reporting approach.

1. *Trusteeship Council and Committee on Information from Non-Self-Governing Territories*

The question of application or extension of "international conventions and agreements" to the Trust and Non-Self-Governing Territories has been periodically reviewed by the Trusteeship Council and the Committee on Information from Non-Self-Governing Territories.

The Trusteeship Council issued a questionnaire requiring States responsible for Trust Territories to furnish data about the law and practices governing human rights, labour and narcotic drugs, among other subjects. The States concerned are also to enumerate the "international treaties, conventions and other agreements applying to the Territory, with an indication which of them have been applied during the year under review."[51]

The Committee on Information from Non-Self-Governing Territories issued a standard form for the guidance of Members in the preparation of information to be transmitted under Article 73(e) of the Charter. The Standard Form states:

> In order to permit the Special Committee to review the progress achieved in the Non-Self-Governing Territories in the fields covered by Article 73 (e) of the Charter, Members are invited to provide a survey of the principles and practical measures showing general trends in the Territories concerned, such as . . . (d) Action for the adoption, ratification or implementation of international agreements of particular concern to the territories.[52]

The data and information supplied by the Administering Authorities in regard to application of "international conventions" is reviewed in the Trusteeship Council and the Committee on Information from Non-Self-Governing Territories. Studies on the progress of the Non-Self-Governing Territories indicate the usefulness of these review procedures.[53]

States had adhered to the 1910 Convention on White Slave Traffic by 1920, the analogous but more comprehensive 1921 Convention received 46 ratifications or accessions by 1934.

[51] U.N. Doc. T/1010. *Questionnaire as Approved by the Trusteeship Council at its 414th Meeting.*

[52] United Nations, *The Standard Form for the Guidance of Members in the Preparation of Information to be Transmitted under Article 73(e) of the Charter,* 1951, p. 3.

[53] On the impact of the review by the Committee on Information from Non-Self-Governing Territories, see United Nations, *Progress of the Non-Self-Governing Territories under the Charter (1961),* vol. 3, p. 149.

2. *Duty of federal States to "report" to their own constituent units*

Some United Nations conventions[54] contain a federal clause which stipulates the following obligations for a federal State party to the convention:

(a) to bring those articles of the convention which for their implementation require legislative action by constituent units (States, provinces or cantons) "with a favourable recommendation to the notice of the appropriate authorities of States, provinces or cantons at the earliest possible moment." It will be noted that this duty to report differs from the analogous provision in the I.L.O. Constitution. Also, this clause neither sets a time limit nor establishes any additional duty, unlike the I.L.O. Constitution,[55] to report to the international organization that sponsored the convention.

(b) to supply at the request of any other Contracting State "a statement of the law and practice of the Federation and its constituent units" showing the "extent to which effect has been given" to any particular provision of the convention by legislative or other action by federal authorities and/or authorities of constituent units.

Metropolitan Governments to secure consent of non-metropolitan Territories

Some conventions (for example, on the Nationality of Married Women, 1957, on the Reduction of Statelessness, 1961, and the Supplementary Slavery Convention, 1956) contain a somewhat more stringent provision regarding application of the convention to dependencies of a Contracting State:

(a) If the consent of the dependency is required by the constitutional laws or practices of the State or the dependency, "that Contracting State shall endeavour to secure the needed consent" of the dependency within twelve months from the date of the signature by the former.

(b) Upon obtaining such consent, the Contracting State shall notify the Secretary-General. In case the consent is not obtained within a twelve-month period, the State "shall inform the Secretary-General of the results of the consultations" with those dependencies "whose consent to the application of the present Convention may have been withheld."

4. *Significance for non-parties of reports by parties about implementation*

Although the question of implementation of conventions by contracting parties is outside the purview of this study, a reference to pro-

---

[54] Refugee Convention, 1951 (art. 41); Refugee Protocol, 1967 (art. VI); Convention relating to the Status of Stateless Persons, 1954 (art. 37); Convention on the Recovery Abroad of Maintenance, 1956 (art. 11).

[55] See below.

visions requiring reports about implementation is warranted because such reports may facilitate the decision for States not yet parties to become parties. For example, the parties to the Supplementary Slavery Convention, 1956, undertook "to communicate to the Secretary-General of the United Nations copies of any laws, regulations and administrative measures enacted or put into effect to implement" it. Such information is then communicated, *inter alia*, to the ECOSOC[56] and thus becomes available to States non-parties, apprising them of what participation in the convention may entail.

C. INTERNATIONAL LABOUR ORGANISATION

The international organization that has from its inception made the widest use of reporting is the International Labour Organisation. This has in part been due to the imaginativeness and daring of the drafters of the I.L.O. Constitution, who recognized that the making of conventions and their widest implementation and acceptance was the principal means of achieving the social welfare objectives of the I.L.O.

1. *The four-fold "reporting system" of the I.L.O.*

I.L.O. members have a four-fold "reporting" duty regarding conventions adopted by the International Labour Conference:

(a) Each member Government[57] is bound, within one year "at

---

[56] Art. 8, paras. 2 and 3; similarly, art. 36 of Refugee Convention, 1955; art. II, para. 2 of Refugee Protocol, 1967; art. 33 of Convention relating to Status of Stateless Persons; art. 18, para. 1(b) of the Single Convention on Narcotic Drugs, 1961, and other narcotic drugs instruments; art. 7 of UNESCO Convention against Discrimination in Education, 1960. See also art. 9 of the Convention on Racial Discrimination, 1965; art. 40 of the Covenant on Civil and Political Rights, 1966; and art. 16 of the Covenant on Economic, Social and Cultural Rights, 1966.

Not all of these instruments refer specifically to the forwarding of the reported information to the ECOSOC, but the information becomes generally available also in the absence of such provisions.

[57] The obligation is unqualified for unitary States and is the same for federal States, whenever the federal Government considers an International Labour convention "appropriate under its constitutional system for federal action." As Oppenheim-Lauterpacht (*International Law*, vol. 1, 8th ed., p. 725) observes, "the test [of 'appropriateness'] is not one of strict legal power but of constitutional propriety."

If, however, a federal Government regards an International Labour convention as "appropriate," in whole or in part, for action by the constituent units (states, provinces or cantons), it must refer the convention to their respective authorities and hold periodic consultations with them, with a view to promoting "co-ordinated" action to give effect to the convention. (International Labour Conference, 29th session (1946), Report II (1), *Reports of the Conference Delegation on Constitutional Questions*, pp. 173-186.) These provisions, introduced in 1946, constitute a tightening of the obligations of federal Governments, because until then the latter could most"[58] after the closing of the conference session that adopted a convention, to do all that is necessary to "bring it before" the country's authority or authorities (usually the legislature) "for the enactment of legislation or other action." This duty exists regardless of whether the Government voted for the convention[59] or even participated in the conference session that adopted it.[60]

(b) Secondly, each Government is required to inform the Director-General of the International Labour Office of the following: (i) the "measures" it has taken in fulfilment of the obligation just mentioned, the broad term "measures" covering any steps required or appropriate pursuant to the country's law and practice (for example, introducing a bill into the lower house of the legislature and, after the latter had passed the bill, convening the upper house); (ii) the "particulars" of the authority or authorities which the Government considered competent to deal with the respective labour convention, which implies that if the Government could have brought the convention before different authorities, the Government is expected to explain its choice to the I.L.O.; (iii) the action taken by the authority (authorites) before which the convention was brought.[61]

(c) Thereafter, the extent and content of the information that the Government has to transmit to the I.L.O. depends on what action that authority or those authorities took.

If the action was positive (in the words of art. 19, para. 5(d) of the I.L.O. Constitution, "if the Member obtains consent" of that authority or those authorities, the Government "will communicate the formal ratification of the Convention to the Director-General."

---

in certain circumstances treat the conventions as if they were recommendations. (See Oppenheim-Lauterpacht, *ibid.*, pp. 725-726 and note 2, p. 726.) International Labour recommendations are instruments adopted by the conference in the same manner as conventions, on matters "not considered suitable or appropriate at that time" for a convention (art. 19, para. 1, I.L.O. Constitution). In view of the far greater number and significance of the I.L.O. conventions than of the I.L.O. recommendations, consideration of the latter instruments is omitted here.

[58] If "it is impossible owing to exceptional circumstances" to meet the one-year deadline, "then at the earliest practicable moment" within a maximum of eighteen months (art. 19, para. 5(b) of the I.L.O. Constitution).

[59] Permanent Court of International Justice, Series B, No. 13, p. 17.

[60] *Cf. International Labour Conference.* Final Record, 3rd session, p. 219.

Mention must also be made of the fact that International Labour Conventions are not signed, and are therefore also not opened for signature. The omission of the signing phase precludes any distinction between signatories and non-signatories and any conclusion to be drawn from non-signature.

[61] Art. 19, para. 5(c).

If the authority or authorities on which the ratification depended acted negatively, or, in the words of para. 5(e), "if the Member does not obtain [their] consent," the Government's duty to report to the I.L.O. continues indefinitely. At appropriate intervals, as requested by the Governing Body, it shall report to the Director-General about its law and practice in regard to the matters dealt with in the convention,[62] and about the difficulties which prevent or delay ratification.

By requesting these periodic reports after a Government's bona fide effort to obtain ratification had failed, the I.L.O. Constitution implies two significant principles. First, in spite of non-ratification, the substance of the convention should still be given at least partial effect, through legislative or administrative action, collective labour contracts or otherwise. Furthermore, even if this is done, the I.L.O. Constitution nevertheless desires the convention's formal ratification and expects the Government to make further efforts toward that end.

(d) After a few years' experience, the International Labour Conference concluded that the system just outlined required further strengthening. In 1926 it established a committee of independent experts[63] which has become a permanent feature of the I.L.O. system.

The Committee is called upon (as stated in a Governing Body resolution of 30 October 1947) "to examine the information and reports concerning Conventions and Recommendations [already] communicated by Members in accordance with Article 19 of the Constitution." In addition, the Committee, on its own initiative or as a result of comments and information it receives from employer and worker organizations, frequently requests the Director-General to obtain further information[64] from Governments.

---

[62] The I.L.O. Constitution specifies in art. 19, para. 5(e), that these reports about "law and practice" shall show "the extent to which effect has been given, or is proposed to be given, to any of the provisions of the [unratified] Convention by legislation, administrative action, collective agreement or otherwise."

[63] Committee of Experts on the Application of [International Labour] Conventions and Recommendations. Instead of the tri-partite (Government, employers, workers) composition characteristic of I.L.O. organs, the Conference resolution establishing the Committee prescribed that its members be chosen for their personal independence and technical competence in labour relations. They are appointed by the I.L.O. Governing Body on the proposal of the Director-General of the International Labour Office.

[64] The Committee has endeavoured to obtain authorization to request the additional information they desire directly from the Governments concerned, but the procedure by which they have to channel those requests through the Director-General has so far not been changed. On the other hand, the Committee always schedules one of its three annual sessions during the all-member International Labour Conference, which enables it to obtain formal and informal information from government, management and labour delegates.

The Committee's main function has been to review the application (implementation) of International Labour conventions in countries that had ratified them. But since the Committee deals with all situations contemplated in Article 19 of the I.L.O. Constitution, it has given the same detailed examination to delays in ratification. As a result of this collection and systematic review of pertinent data regarding delayed ratifications, the Committee of Experts has been able to suggest remedial measures, when suitable, for the consideration of the Governments and the I.L.O.

At each annual session of the International Labour Conference, these matters are also examined by a Conference committee which, unlike the committee of independent experts, is composed of government, employer and employee members chosen by the Conference. This Confer_ence Committee on the Application of [International Labour] Conventions and Recommendations primarily examines the effect (implementation) given by members to conventions already ratified by them. But like the parallel experts committee, it is also required to deal with pending and delayed ratifications.[65] For this it considers the information previously available to the experts committee and the reports of the latter, as well as supplementary information provided to it (usually at the respective session of the International Labour Conference) by government, employer or employee representatives, whether in support of or opposition to the findings of the experts. Thus, the review by the tri-partite conference committee adds "a certain dynamic impulse" to the consideration by the Committee of Experts.

The fact that some essential "human rights" standards laid down in international treaties are considered to be applicable also for States not parties to them is illustrated by the competence of the I.L.O. Committee on Freedom of Association.

2. The I.L.O. Committee on Freedom of Association[66]

This separate committee deals with complaints by Governments or by employers or workers organizations relating to freedom of association of these organizations. "It must be emphasized that complaints relating to freedom of association may be presented even against States which are not formally bound by the conventions on freedom and association."[67]

Between 1951 and 1965, the Committee examined over 450 cases,

---

[65] G.B. 103/12/6, pp. 11-13.

[66] Created in 1951 by the Governing Body of the I.L.O. in agreement with the Economic and Social Council, it consists of three government, three employers and three workers members.

[67] Report by the I.L.O. to the 40th session of ECOSOC, published in *Official Records of the ECOSOC, 40th session, Annexes,* agenda item 9, Doc. E/4144, p. 25.

and a number of those pertained to States not parties to the conventions on freedom of association.[68]

D. OTHER SPECIALIZED AGENCIES

1. *UNESCO*

The UNESCO Constitution provides for procedures to promote and expedite ratifications which to some extent resemble the analogous I.L.O. procedures. Each member State must submit UNESCO conventions and recommendations to its competent authority (or authorities) within one year from the close of the General Conference session at which they were adopted (art. IV, para. 4), and they must report periodically to the Organization, in a manner to be determined by the Conference, on the action taken upon these instruments (art. VIII).

Pursuant to the latter provision, the General Conference determined[69] that initial special reports relating to any such instrument shall be transmitted not less than two months prior to the opening of the first ordinary session of the General Conference following the session at which it was adopted.

In 1958, the General Conference determined the substance of the initial reports. They must include: (a) a statement indicating whether the convention or recommendation has been submitted to the competent national authority (or authorities); (b) the name(s) of the authority (authorities); (c) a statement indicating whether any steps have been taken by the authority (authorities) to give effect to the instrument; and (d) the nature of such steps.[70]

After considering these reports, the Conference is to submit its observations in one or more general reports of its own to member States,

---

[68] *Ibid.*, p. 26.
Regarding the results, this I.L.O. report states:
On many occasions the Governing Body, on the proposal of the Committee, has addressed recommendations to Governments to amend their national law or practice. In an appreciable number of cases, the Governments of the countries concerned have had regard to these recommendations. In particular, effect has been given to recommendations of the Governing Body in the following ways: legislation which was criticized has been repealed or amended, practices considered to be incompatible with the principles of freedom of association have been abandoned, factual situations which gave rise to complaints have been remedied, imprisoned trade union leaders have been released, death sentences passed on trade unionists have been commuted.

[69] Rules of Procedure concerning recommendations to Member States and international conventions, adopted in 1950, reproduced in *Official Records of the ECOSOC, 40th session, Annexes,* agenda item 9, U.N. Doc. E/4133, p .2.

[70] *Ibid.*

to the National Commissions for UNESCO and to any other authorities it may designate. The General Conference adopted a resolution in 1966 urging member States to become parties to UNESCO conventions.[71]

2. *World Health Organization*

According to article 20 of the W.H.O. Constitution, each Member "undertakes that it will, within eighteen months after the adoption by the Health Assembly of a Convention or agreement, take action relating to [its] acceptance . . . Each Member shall notify the Director-General of the action taken and if it does not accept such convention or agreement within the time-limit, it will furnish a statement of the reasons for non-acceptance. . . ."[72]

III. INFORMATION, ADVICE AND ASSISTANCE BY INTERNATIONAL ORGANIZATIONS

International organizations can more or less directly further the acceptance of treaties with which they are concerned by a variety of other methods, ranging from dissemination of basic information about those instruments to advice and assistance to Governments. It should be noted that so far, the extent and character of these activities have been left mainly to the discretion of the respective Secretariats.

A. DISSEMINATION OF INFORMATION ABOUT TREATIES

1. *United Nations Secretariat*

Factual information about United Nations treaties is made available in several ways. If a new treaty is adopted by a conference, the text is immediately reproduced in the conference records.[73] If it is adopted by the General Assembly itself, the resolution bearing the text will at once appear in the Assembly documents. The United Nations Office of Public

---

[71] See res. No. 39.2, adopted during the 14th session, with regard to the Convention against Discrimination in Education, 1960, and the Protocol Instituting a Conciliation and Good Offices Commission to be responsible for seeking a settlement of any disputes which may arise between States parties to the Convention against Discrimination in Education (1962).

[72] No convention or agreement has been adopted by the Health Assembly; thus there has been no occasion to apply art. 20. However, the Health Assembly in its 2nd, 3rd, 8th and 12th sessions adopted resolutions urging members not yet parties to the Convention on Privileges and Immunities of the Specialized Agencies to accede to it (W.H.O., *Hand Book of Resolutions and Decisions of the World Health Assembly and the Executive Board* (1967), p. 303 ff).

[73] Information about the developments that led to the adoption of the text (debates at the Conference showing attitudes of different Governments; amendments, with reasons for their acceptance or rejection; detailed voting record and other data often required for detailed analysis) can also be found in the Conference records.

Information may, subject to budget and other considerations, subsequently publish it in pamphlet form.[74] After an unavoidable lapse of time, the text is reproduced in the *United Nations Yearbook* (which will also contain a summary of the treaty's evolution), in the *U.N. Juridical Yearbook* and in the *Treaty Series* of the United Nations.

Whenever a State signs, ratifies, accedes or succeeds to a multilateral treaty for which the Secretary-General acts as depositary, all concerned Governments are advised thereof by circular note.

Comprehensive information on all those treaties is contained in a periodic United Nations publication, now titled *Status of Multilateral Treaties in respect of which the Secretary-General Performs Depositary Functions.* It includes dates of signatures, ratifications, accessions; notifications on succession; dates of entry into force; the texts of reservations, declarations, objections to reservations, and instruments concerning territorial application. The publication now[75] consists of one bound volume to be issued annually and containing all data about treaties except final clauses. It includes a separate loose-leaf "Annex" containing final clauses, which is published less often but supplemented by loose leaves.[76]

The U.N. Yearbook on Human Rights contains a considerable quantity of material (including, for example, texts of national statutes parallel to or issued pursuant to a United Nations human rights convention) that may be useful to Governments examining such a convention. However, because of its comprehensiveness, the Yearbook cannot be up to date. Some of the volumes in the United Nations *Legislative Series* offer texts and other pertinent information on bilateral treaties and other instruments on topics covered by United Nations conventions.

The section on "Treaties and Multilateral Conventions" in the *Annual Report of the Secretary-General on the Work of the Organization* furnishes summary information about the number of treaties registered with the Secretariat, new multilateral treaties concluded under United

---

[74] For example, the pamphlet "The Crime of Genocide—a United Nations convention aimed at preventing destruction of groups and at punishing those responsible" (OPI/208, 6th rev.ed., 1965) gives the full text of the Genocide Convention, summarizes it in a few pages and refers to its "Prospects," stating (p. 7):

> Throughout the world, people aware of the importance and vital necessity of the Genocide Convention are working for its acceptance. The basis of their support transcends religious beliefs and crosses political lines.

[75] The original design of this publication was to bring out one main volume (they appeared in 1949, 1952 and 1959) and to update it through loose-leaf supplements. The 1968 edition (ST/LEG/SER.D/1) started the new design, because the arrangement proved "not entirely suitable." (See ST/LEG/SER.D/1, p. xiii.)

[76] In 1968, it was announced that these leaves will also reproduce the full texts of future treaties for which the Secretary-General will be depositary.

Nations auspices and the status of signatures, ratifications and accessions, including entry into force, of the multilateral treaties for which the Secretary-General exercises depositary functions.[77]

Non-technical summaries of United Nations conventions, and sometimes their texts, are published in the *U.N. Monthly Chronicle* and, as mentioned before, in brochures published by the Office of Public Information.

Finally, the Office of Public Information and the United Nations Information Centres issue periodic press releases on the status of multilateral treaties. Information about certain of the major treaties has also been disseminated through radio broadcasts.

2. *Background papers on treaties*

On occasion, the United Nations Secretariat provides descriptions, usually issued as mimeographed documents, of the evolution, objectives and contents of major United Nations treaties.[78]

A special study, prepared by the Secretariat, regarding succession of States to multilateral treaties, is furnished to "new" States at the time of eliciting information about successions.[79]

3. *International Labour Office*

Two of the publication activities of the I.L.O. may be singled out. It makes available the texts of all International Labour conventions and recommendations, together with information about their ratifications and other pertinent matters, within a single volume, *The International Labour Code.* Also, it publishes biannually a large single-sheet *Chart of Ratifications* of its conventions that shows at a glance (a) for each of the over 100 conventions, which members have accepted it, and (b) for each member State, which of all those conventions it has accepted.[80]

---

[77] The Revised General Act for the Pacific Settlement of International Disputes, 1949, provides (art. 43, para. 3) that the three lists showing the three forms of accessions permitted by it, and additional declarations of the contracting parties, shall be continually kept up to date and published in the Secretary-General's annual report to the General Assembly.

[78] See, among others, *Measures taken within the United Nations in the Field of Human Rights* (A/CONF.32/5) and *Methods used by the United Nations in the Field of Human Rights* (A/CONF.32/6). *The Work of the International Law Commission* (printed as U.N. Publication 67.V.4) also contains pertinent information.

[79] See A/CN.4/150, printed in the *Yearbook of the International Law Commission* (1962), vol. II, pp. 106-131.

[80] The publication of tables and graphs showing signatures and ratifications was strongly recommended in 1930 also for conventions adopted under the auspices of the League of Nations by a League Committee which observed that the graphic form "will materially assist in enlightening public opinion." (L.o.N. Doc. A.10.1930.V, p. 4.)

(Regarding this Committee, and other recommendations by it, see above.)

Both publications have proved very useful to members. Representatives of States with whom discussions were held observed that the chart mentioned helps to foster acceptance of I.L.O. conventions.

It is debatable and also unimportant whether a particular international activity on behalf of conventions constitutes dissemination of factual information or solicitation and exhortation. The important fact is that wide dissemination, easy availability, clear presentation and constant updating of all pertinent information are basic requirements for wider acceptance of international conventions.

B. ADVICE CONCERNING TREATIES

1. *International officials*

As a general principle, and for various reasons, the legal offices of the United Nations and specialized agencies do not furnish Members with official advice or interpretation regarding multilateral treaties. However, officials of the organizations are available for consultation, and the secretariats of some of the organizations also furnish written replies to inquiries from Member Governments.[81]

Furthermore, there are occasions when international officials are in a position to encourage the application of standards set by international conventions or to discuss some objective consequences of their acceptance and non-acceptance. Since the I.L.O. is the agency concerned about the largest number of conventions, informal interviews were held with I.L.O. officials, who indicate that the following methods, among others, have been adopted: I.L.O. experts rendering advisory services to members are required to act in conformity with the standards set by I.L.O. conventions and recommendations and, when suitable, to draw the attention of members to the need and desirability of ratifying particular conventions. Furthermore, the senior I.L.O. staff is encouraged, when on official travel

---

[81] As regards, for example, International Labour conventions, such "advice is always available and regularly sought [from the International Labour Office] when Governments contemplating ratification require clarification of the meaning of a Convention." (E. A. Landy, *The Effectiveness of International Supervision* (New York, 1966), p. 90.) "An average of four to five such interpretations are supplied each year and published in the [I.L.O.] *Official Bulletin*; the explanations are therefore available not only to the governments which asked for them but to other countries as well." (Landy, *op. cit.*, p. 90, fn. 3.) *Cf.* in this connexion C. Wilfred Jenks, "The interpretation of international labour conventions by the International Labour Office," *British Yearbook of International Law*, vol. 20 (1939), pp. 132-142.

Furthermore, "The secretariat of every general session of the International Labour Conference includes a 'Conventions Information Unit' whose services are . . . available to 'members of delegations wishing to discuss questions concerning the ratification of Conventions and related matters.' Regular use is made of these facilities, particularly by delegates from the newly independent countries." Landy *op. cit.*, p. 90, fn. 4.

or home leave, to meet with representatives of members and to render such assistance as may alleviate difficulties regarding ratification of a particular convention or conventions.[82] Third, whenever it comes to their knowledge that a member State has come very close to ratifying a convention but that some technical difficulty has proved an obstacle, I.L.O. officials would assist in removing it.

2. *International Bureau for the Protection of Intellectual Property* (BIRPI)

Some activities of the International Bureau for the Protection of Intellectual Property (BIRPI), which is mainly concerned with the proper functioning of the Paris Convention for the Protection of Industrial Property, 1883, and the Berne Convention for the Protection of Literary and Artistic Works, 1886, are not dissimilar from those just mentioned. Informal discussions with BIRPI officials have disclosed that visits by senior staff members of the Bureau to national capitals, as well as consultations with the competent authorities on problems regarding acceptance, the preparation of model laws and special training programmes on the legal problems involved have helped to facilitate wider acceptance by States of their conventions.[83]

3. *International Court of Justice*

Pursuant to Article 96 of the Charter of the United Nations, the General Assembly and other organs of the United Nations and specialized agencies so authorized by the Assembly may request the Court to give an advisory opinion on "any" legal question, and therefore also on legal questions concerning a convention adopted under their respective auspices.[84] Pursuant to the I.L.O. Constitution (article 37, paragraph 1), the Court can be asked for authoritative interpretation of international labour conventions. The I.L.O. Governing Body invoked the provision in

---

[82] Mr. Albert Thomas, the first Director-General of the I.L.O., considered the promotion of acceptances of International Labour conventions as one of his important responsibilities during his visit to the capitals of member States. I.L.O., *International Social Policy* (Geneva, 1948), pp. 14, 15 and 16. Also, more recently the Director-General has been required by decisions of the Governing Body to promote the ratification of I.L.O. conventions. (See, e.g., Minutes of the 147th session of the Governing Body, Fourth sitting, p. 30 and appen. V, paras. 24-26, for recommendations in regard to Discrimination (Employment and Occupation) Convention, 1958.)

[83] At present, the number of States parties to the Paris Convention is 79, and to the Berne Convention, 59.

[84] See request by General Assembly of 16 November 1950, for advisory opinion on three questions concerning reservations to the Genocide Convention, and the Court's advisory opinion of 28 May 1952. *I.C.J. Reports 1951*, p. 15.

1932, asking the Permanent Court of International Justice to give an interpretation of the Night Work (Women) Convention, 1919.[85]

4. *General conclusions adopted by I.L.O. Committee of Experts*

More use has been made under the practice of the I.L.O. of a non-judicial device. The I.L.O. Committee of (independent) Experts adopts, when appropriate, "General Conclusions" after examining reports of Governments which have and have not ratified certain I.L.O. conventions. These opinions do not possess binding or authoritative character but are subsequently discussed by the tripartite I.L.O. Conference Committee. The device is described by one commentator as being "designed to clarify the terms and bearing of the instruments examined and thus to help Governments in determining whether to ratify."[86]

5. *United Nations High Commissioner for Refugees* (UNHCR)

The widest functions regarding specific treaties, including advisory functions but going beyond them, have been assigned by the General Assembly to this body. The Statute of the Office of the United Nations High Commissioner for Refugees enumerates a variety of ways by which the High Commissioner "shall provide for the protection of refugees falling under the competence of his Office." The list starts by directing him to do so by

promoting the conclusion and ratification of international conventions for the protection of refugees, supervising their application and proposing amendments thereto.[87]

The term "High Commissioner," as used in the Statute, covers, as appropriate, UNHCR staff members in addition to the head of UNHCR.

Under this mandate, UNHCR has offered assistance to Governments on questions concerning ratification of or accession to the Refugee Convention, 1951, and the Protocol relating to the Status of Refugees. In their visits to national capitals, the High Commissioner and senior UNHCR officers have constantly brought the Convention and the Pro-

---

[85] Landy, *op. cit.,* p. 90, fn. 2.

[86] Landy, *ibid.*, fn.1, citing as example that India, after originally deciding not to ratify a Convention (No. 100), did so when one of its Labour Ministry's Committees re-examined it on the basis of the explanation by the I.L.O. Expert Committee.

[87] Art. 8(a) of the Statute (Assembly res. 428 (V) of 14 December 1950). This provision also covers the right of UNHCR to take positions towards Member Governments regarding legal interpretation of international conventions for the protection of refugees. (See, e.g., concerning the interpretation by the UNHCR Regional Representative of the applicability of the Refugee Convention, 1951, to Jamaica pursuant to a United Kingdom-Jamaica devolution agreement, Legal Opinion of the United Nations Secretariat of 5 March 1963, *United Nations Juridical Yearbook* (1963), pp. 181-2.)

tocol, since the latter has been open for accession, to the attention of Governments, with a view to securing their acceptance. By 31 December 1968, 54 States were parties to the Convention. The Protocol, opened for accession only on 31 January 1967, had received 9 acceptances by the end of 1967, and that number had increased to 28 one year later.

One factor contributing to the comparatively large number of acceptances by African States has been the role played by representatives of various UNHCR Offices in Africa.[88]

Especially since early 1967, when the Protocol made the Convention applicable also to persons who became refugees as a result of contemporary events, the gain in adherences to both instruments has indicated the usefulness of promotional activities regarding acceptance.

6. *Special rapporteurs*

Acceptance of treaties can also be promoted, although evidently only indirectly, by the work of special rapporteurs appointed by a United Nations organ to investigate a particular problem. For example, the Special Rapporteur on Slavery formulated with Secretariat assistance a detailed questionnaire on slavery which was sent in fall 1964 to all Member States. Among numerous other questions, it asked:

If your country is not yet a party to the International Slavery Convention of 1926 or the Supplementary Convention of 1956:

(1) Does it contemplate becoming a party to either or both Conventions, and, if so, when?

(2) What steps have been taken with a view to ratification of, or accession to, either or both Conventions, such as bringing any of them before the authority or authorities within whose competence the matter lies for enactment of legislation or other action? What have been the results?

(3) What obstacles or impediments delay or prevent ratification of, or accession to, either or both Conventions? Under what conditions would ratification of, or accession to, either or both Conventions be possible?[89]

In their replies, some Governments explained that there was no slavery or slavery-type institution or practice in their countries; others stated that measures had been initiated with a view to ratifying the conventions.

---

[88] As of 31 December 1968, of the 39 States in Africa, 22 were parties to the Convention and 10 to the Protocol.

Even three years earlier, the General Assembly expressed satisfaction that the African States are showing a continuing interest in the problems of refugees by generously receiving refugees in a truly humanitarian spirit and by acceding in increasing numbers to the 1951 Convention relating to the Status of Refuges. (Res. 2040 (XX) of 7 December 1965.)

[89] United Nations, *Report on Slavery* by Mohamed Awad, Special Rapporteur on Slavery (1966) (E/4168/Rev. 1), p. 263.

It is noteworthy that since the questionnaire was sent out, the Supplementary Slavery Convention has gained acceptance from 8 additional States; currently, it has 73 parties. The conclusion is perhaps permitted that the attention which the detailed questionnaire engendered, not only towards that treaty but towards the many aspects of the subject matter, contributed to this development.

C. INTERNATIONAL TECHNICAL ASSISTANCE

Various assistance and development activities of the United Nations system can indirectly contribute to the wider acceptance of treaties, by helping overcome obstacles, especially in developing States, that prevent their Governments from adhering to treaties they consider desirable. If, for example, implementation of such a convention would make demands on public administration which the country cannot yet fulfil, the advisory services, training and research of the United Nations Programme in Public Administration or the advisory services and fellowships in public administration under General Assembly resolution 723 (VIII) may promote acceptance of the convention.

The difficulties may also be due to insufficient legal expertise for the evaluation of the instruments in question or for the drafting of implementary domestic legislation and regulations. Some international technical assistance designed to strengthen legal expertise has been provided.

1. *Experts and legal advisers*

The services of experts and legal advisers are made available by the United Nations through the Office of Technical Co-operation, either under the technical assistance component of the United Nations Development Programme (UNDP) or the regular programme of the United Nations.[90] The Secretary-General has drawn the attention of the UNDP resident representatives to the availability of this form of assistance.[91] In 1965-1966, twelve requests were submitted for the services of experts in such fields as transport agreements, air law, maritime law, "United Nations income-tax legislation," and others.[92] For the period 1967-1968, the number of analogous requests rose to twenty-five. One of the latter specifically related to United Nations international treaties; others referred to air law, "United Nations taxation treaties," and similar fields.[93]

By 1968, three Governments obtained the services of legal advisers

[90] See Res. 2204 (XXI).

[91] See *Official Records of the General Assembly, 22nd session, Annexes,* agenda item 90, Doc. A/6816, p. 5.

[92] *Ibid.,* p. 6. The twelve requests amounted cumulatively to 149 man-months. In response, legal experts were supplied in four cases, for a total of thirty man-months.

[93] *Ibid.*

under the so-called OPEX programme (Programme for the Provision of Operational, Executive and Administrative Personnel). The main difference between OPEX personnel and other technical assistance experts is that OPEX experts are in charge of operational, executive or administrative functions (or, as in the case of legal advisers, perform other sensitive functions) on behalf of the Government to which they are assigned. They are therefore under the control and discipline of that Government, with the understanding that their functions be compatible with and in furtherance of the principles and purposes of the international organization that provides their services. Furthermore, OPEX personnel are especially required to train local personnel, the assumption being that "understudies" are best trained "on the job."[94]

Among the experts in the field of human rights whose services are provided under an Assembly resolution of 1956,[95] two have been concerned with matters pertaining to election laws and to the status of women.

2. *Training activities*

The training activities of the United Nations, UNITAR and UNESCO in the field of international law aim at deepening participants' expertise in multilateral treaties. The 1967 regional training and refresher course in international law, held in Tanzania, [96] discussed among other questions the acceptance by African States of certain codification and human rights conventions. One of the topics of the 1968 regional seminar in international law, held in Quito, Ecuador, was "Regional problems arising out of treaties relating to the resources of the sea."[97]

3. *International Law Fellowships*

The International Law Fellowships programme of the United Nations, UNITAR and UNESCO has provided opportunities for personnel from developing countries to study questions connected with acceptance of United Nations treaties and to discuss related legal problems with United Nations officials.[98]

---

[94] *Official Records of the General Assembly, 14th session, Annexes,* agenda item 31, U.N. Doc. A/4212 and Add. 1 (provision of operational, executive and administrative personnel: Report of the Secretary-General).

[95] U.N. Doc. A/CONF.32/6, p. 176, referring to res. 926 (X).

[96] The training course was organized in pursuance of G.A. res. 2204 (XXI).

[97] *Official Records of the ECOSOC, 46th session, Annexes,* agenda item 16, Doc. E/4622.

[98] In 1968 the United Nations awarded fifteen international law fellowships. The Secretary-General stated in his report to the General Assembly that the United Nations international law fellowship scheme should be maintained in close cooperation with UNITAR on the same lines as in 1968. See U.N. Doc. A/6816, *ibid.*, p. 10.

4. *Register of experts and scholars in international law*

Mention may also be made of the "Register of experts and scholars in the field of international law" issued by the United Nations Secretariat in July 1967 (A/6677). It contains the names of and pertinent data about specialists in the teaching and practice of international law, provided by Member Governments, and it can be helpful to States wishing to secure the services of experts and legal advisers on treaty questions.

IV. REVIEW OR REVISION OF TREATIES

A. HOLDING OF NEW INTERNATIONAL CONFERENCES

If, after a certain period of time, no ratifications of a convention are forthcoming, or if their number is very small, it may be desirable to hold a new conference with a view to amending the convention.

Proposal of League of Nations Committee, 1930

The 1930 Report of the League Committee, mentioned before, went so far as to recommend that the following be written into all future general conventions concluded under League auspices:

> It should be provided with regard to any future general convention concluded under the auspices of the League that if, at the end of a certain period to be fixed by the Conference there were not a certain number of States bound by the convention (the number would also be fixed by the Conference, and ought as a rule to be greater than the number actually necessary to bring the convention into force), a meeting of all the signatories (to which other non-signatory States might perhaps be invited to attend) should be convened to examine the position, study the reasons why the ratifications have not been forthcoming, and consider if it would not be well to amend the convention in certain particulars with a view to bringing it more fully into line with the requirements of the greatest possible number of countries.[99]

The recommendation adds that such a provision should not be embodied in the convention itself, because if insufficient ratification prevents it from entering into force, this provision would also remain without effect. Hence, the agreement to hold a subsequent conference, if one is needed, should be written in a separate instrument (for example, the Protocol of Signature) which is not subject to ratification.[100]

---

[99] *Ibid.*, League of Nations Doc. A.10.1930.V, p. 6.

[100] The 1930 Report of the League Committee annexed the following draft for such agreement:

> If on . . . (date) the said Convention is not in force with regard to . . . Members of the League of Nations and non-Member States, the Secretary-General of the League shall request the Council to convene a conference of all the Members of the League of Nations and non-Member States on whose behalf the Convention has been signed or accessions thereto deposited to consider the situation, and the Government of every Member or non-Member State aforesaid

B. REVISION OF INTERNATIONAL LABOUR CONVENTIONS

The International Labour Organisation has adopted several "revised" conventions regarding subject matttrs for which previous conevntions had proved unsuccessful. For example:

No. 28—Protection against Accidents (Dockers, 1929), which obtained only four ratifications, was followed by a revised Convention of the same name (No. 32—1932), which obtained 16 ratifications by 1 April 1954 and twenty-nine by 31 December 1968.

No. 31—Hours of Work (Coal Mines, 1931), which received two ratifications, was followed by a revised Convention of the same name (No. 46—1935), faring not much better (two ratifications by 31 December 1968).

No. 66—Migration for Employment (1939) remained altogether unratified. It was followed by a revised Convention of the same name (No. 97—1949), ratified by eight Members as of 1 April 1954 and by twenty-nine as of 31 December 1968.

The "try and try again" approach has been used, in particular by the Maritime Sessions of the International Labour Conference. The basic Hours of Work (Industry) Convention of 1919 that established the eight-hour work day and the six-day work week, specifically excluded the merchant marine. After years of preparation, the Maritime Conference adopted in 1946 a limited Convention (No. 76) on Wages, Hours of Work and Manning (Sea). When it received only one ratification, the Conference followed it by two revised Conventions, both of the same name (No. 76—1946 and No. 93—1949). However, they had obtained only one and five ratifications, respectively, as of 31 December 1968, so that none of the three instruments has come into force. Hence even in 1958 the Maritime Conference further revised the 1949 Convention, permitting States to exclude the latter's minimum wage provisions for seafarers from ratification, but again without success. Similarly, after the Paid Vacations (Seafarers) Convention (No. 72 of 1946) failed, with three ratifications, to come into effect, the Maritime Conference adopted a more extensively revised Convention on the same subject (No. 91 of 1949).[101] The latter had obtained nine ratifications by the end of 1962 and fifteen by the end of 1968, which still did not include the nine specified maritime States whose ratifications are needed to bring the Convention into force.

The International Labour Conference has also revised certain con-

---

undertakes to be represented at any conference so convened. (*Ibid.*, p. 9.)

[101] The 1946 Convention (No. 72) provides for minimum annual paid vacations of eighteen working days for ship's masters and officers and twelve working days for other crew members. The 1949 Convention (No. 91) makes pay for such vacations optional rather than obligatory.

ventions for the opposite purpose, namely, to improve upon previous conventions, rather than dilute them.[102] This device has been used when the previous less exacting convention had come into effect but when the Conference felt that the aims could be higher.[103]

This device of offering a choice between more exacting (up-to-date) and less exacting (gradually obsolescent) standards has proved more successful than has the opposite device of diluting revision. For example, by the end of 1968, of the three Conventions aimed at placing greater limitations on night work of women (No. 4—1919, No. 41—1934, No. 89—1948), the 1919 Convention was in force in four countries, the 1934 Convention in thirty-six countries and the 1948 Convention in forty-eight countries.

C. United Nations

The United Nations has also under certain circumstances sponsored the adoption of international instruments that would deal more comprehensively with topics already covered by previous conventions, especially in the fields of narcotic drugs and slavery.

The intention of the subsequent treaty to build on the foundation of the previous treaty is expressed clearly in the preamble to the Supplementary Convention on Slavery, 1956. The preamble declares that the preceding Slavery Convention 1926 (to which the 1956 Convention is "supplementary") promoted progress towards the abolition of slavery, but that slavery had not yet been eliminated, and that therefore the 1926 Convention "should now be augmented"[104] by a supplementary conven-

---

[102] For example, the I.L.O. Penal Sanctions (Indigenous Workers) Convention, 1939, provides for immediate abolition of penal sanctions for breaches of labour contracts by non-adult indigenous workers, but only for abolition "progressively and as soon as possible" in the case of adults. It was followed by the Abolition of Penal Sanctions (Indigenous Workers) Convention, 1955, providing for the complete abolition of penal sanctions. (*Cf.* United Nations, *Progress of the Non-Self Governing Territories under the Charter* (1961), vol. 3, p. 142.)

Similarly, the Convention on Fee-Charging Employment Agencies, 1933, which aims at preventing exploitation of job-seekers and obtained 10 ratifications, was followed by a revised and more comprehensive Convention (No. 96—1949) on the same subject which had received 28 ratifications by the end of 1968.

[103] Since the previous Convention with lower standards remained in force, States could still ratify it rather than the new one; or, when ratifying the latter, they could denounce the old one.

[104] In fact, the 1926 League of Nations Slavery Convention was itself an "augmentation" of the 1919 Slavery Convention of Saint Germain-ene-Laye, which in turn was "augmentation" of the anti-slavery Brussels Act of 1890 (see preamble to the 1926 Convention). The United Nations Supplementary Convention of 1956 is therefore the fourth international treaty in a gradually ascending international effort to end slavery.

tion designed to intensify national as well as international efforts toward the abolition of slavery. . . ." Because the 1926 Convention is supplemented by the 1956 Convention, the latter underscores that the former "remains operative,"[105] meaning that States should preferably be parties to both, but could be parties to either.

D. SUBSEQUENT CONFERENCE TO DETERMINE A CONVENTION'S ENTRY INTO FORCE

A device used in the case of one League of Nations convention consists in omitting within the treaty itself the conditions to be fulfilled (number of ratifications) in order to come into effect. Instead, for the Commercial Convention of 24 March 1930, these conditions were determined by a subsequent conference held some seven months after the end of the conference that had adopted it.[106]

E. AVOIDANCE OF CONFERENCE METHOD

The Refugee Convention 1951 is only applicable to persons who have become refugees as a result of events occurring before 1 January 1951 (art. 1A (2)). Thus it also covers persons who became refugees after 1 January 1951, as long as the events causing them to become refugees occurred before that date. But as time progressed and as new refugee situations arose, it proved "increasingly difficult if not impossible for Governments to recognise the existence of such a long-term historical causal link,"[107] so that the Convention was not of direct interest to Governments concerned with contemporary refugee problems, and acceptance of the Convention ebbed.

The situation was eventually remedied not by the making of a new convention or a revision of the existing convention,[108] but by a protocol to it.

The procedure by which the protocol was adopted avoided the conference method. An unofficial "Colloquium on Legal Aspects of Refugee Problems," held in Bellagio, Italy, 21-28 April 1965,[109] agreed that the best and fastest way of removing the January 1951 cut-off date was through a protocol to the Convention; such an instrument was then

---

[105] Para. 7 of preamble to 1956 Supplementary Convention on Slavery.

[106] League of Nations Doc. A.10.1930.V, p. 8.

[107] UNHCR Doc. A/AC.96/346, p. 1.

[108] The Refugee Convention 1951 itself is based on the consideration "that it [was] desirable to revise and consolidate previous international agreements relating to the status of refugees and to extend the scope of and the protection accorded by such instrument by means of a new agreement" (preamble, para. 3).

[109] The Colloquium of nineteen legal experts was sponsored by the Carnegie Endowment for International Peace in consultation with UNHCR (A/AC.96/INF.40). For list of participants, see A/AC.96/INF.40, annex I.

drafted. The Executive Committee of the High Commissioner's Programme amended the draft, then unanimously adopted the final text of the "Protocol relating to the Status of Refugees."[110]

After its approval by ECOSOC (res. 1186 (XLI) on 18 November 1966), it was noted on 16 December 1966 by the General Assembly, which also requested the Secretary-General to transmit the protocol to the States eligible pursuant to the protocol's own provision concerning accession, "with a view to enabling them to accede to the Protocol" (res. 2198 (XXI)).

V. OTHER DEVICES

A. Adjustment of Treaties by an International Organ

By virtue of Section 36 of the Convention on the Privileges and Immunities of the United Nations, 1946, the Secretary-General may conclude with any Member or Members supplementary agreements adjusting the provisions of this Convention so far as that Member or those Members are concerned. These supplementary agreements shall in each case be subject to the approval of the General Assembly.

B. Conclusion of Special Agreements by an International Organ

Article 8(b) of the Statute of the Office of the UNHCR directs the High Commissioner to promote "through special agreements with Governments the execution of any measures calculated to improve the situation of refugees and to reduce the number requiring protection." Hence, the High Commissioner has the authority, which he has occasionally made use of, to conclude such special agreements without putting in motion the United Nations conference machinery, and to choose for them forms which, under the constitutional law of the country concerned, do not require ratification.

C. Continued Participation in a Treaty and Continued Membership in International Organization Dependent upon Ratification of Amendment to its Constitution

The Chicago Convention on International Civil Aviation, 1944, provides that any amendment to it shall come into force only "in respect of States which have ratified such amendment" (art. 94(a)). However, the Convention authorizes the I.C.A.O. Assembly, if in the Assembly's "opinion the amendment is of such a nature as to justify this course," to resolve "that any State which has not ratified within a specified period

---

[110] The method of a protocol had been considered appropriate in view of the urgent need for a simple and rapid solution, which was also relevant as regards the procedure for the protocol's adoption. (See A/AC.96/346, p. 3.)

after the amendment has come into force shall thereupon cease to be a member of the Organization and a party to the Convention" (art. 94(b)).

D. RESTRICTING THE RIGHT OF VOTE OF MEMBER STATES NOT PARTIES TO A TREATY

The Chicago Convention on International Civil Aviation, 1944, also contains another less far-reaching provision. It enjoins the I.C.A.O. to carry out not only the functions placed upon it by this Convention itself, but also the functions placed upon it by two other treaties, the International Air Services Transit Agreement and the International Air Transport Agreement, both of 1944 (art. 66(a)). However, States which "have not accepted" either or both of these treaties "shall not have the right to vote [in the I.C.A.O. Assembly or Council] on any questions referred to the Assembly or Council under the provisions of" these treaties, respectively (art. 66(b)).

E. SUBSTANTIVE TREATY PROVISIONS DESIGNED TO INDUCE STATES' ACCESSIONS

The Single Convention on Narcotic Drugs, 1961, permits States to reserve the right to trade in specified narcotic substances for specified uses and specified periods of time, but with the proviso that such trade must never include export to a non-party (art. 49, paras. 1 and 2(b)). Hence, if a non-party wished to import such products from a party, it would have to become a party to the Convention. Similarly, States parties must in principle[111] not import opium from any non-party; such country would have to accept the Convention before selling opium to any State party, under the conditions set forth in the Convention (art. 24, para. 4(a)). Furthermore, if the International Narcotics Control Board "has reason to believe that the aims of this Convention [limitation and control of production of narcotic substances and prevention, regulation and supervision of illicit traffic in them] are being seriously endangered by reason of the failure of any country to carry out the provisions of this Convention," the Board may "call upon the Government concerned to adopt . . . remedial measures"; if the Government fails to comply, the Board may recommend to parties that they stop the import and/or export of drugs from or to the respective country (art. 14, paras. 1, 2).

---

[111] The exception is that parties "may import opium produced by any country [including any non-party] which produced and exported opium during the ten years prior to 1 January 1961 if such country has established and maintains a national control organ or agency for the purpose set out in article 23 [designation of plots where opium poppy for the production of opium may be cultivated; licensing of cultivators; cultivators must deliver their opium crop to the control agency, which must have a trading monopoly] and has in force an effective means of ensuring that the opium it produces is not diverted into illicit traffic" (art. 24, para. 4(b)).

The provisions of the Convention here summarized do not, of course, impose legal obligations upon non-parties, but are designed to make them follow the main standards accepted as obligations by the parties. This can be considered an indirect inducement to non-parties to become parties and thus also to enjoy the rights which the Convention bestows on parties.

F. OTHER PREROGATIVES LIMITED TO STATES PARTIES

The Convention on Racial Discrimination provides (a) for the establishment of a committee to deal with reports and complaints about the subject matter of the Convention; (b) that only nationals of States parties to the Convention may serve on it; and (c) that only such States may participate in the election of the members of that committee.[112] It is also to be noted that the Committee on the Elimination of Racial Discrimination is to deal with petitions and reports on matters "directly related to the principles and objectives of this Convention" regarding territories to which General Assembly resolution 1514 (XV) applies (article 15 of the Convention).

G. INTERNATIONAL ORGANIZATION CARRYING OUT FUNCTIONS INCUMBENT UPON STATES PARTIES TO A TREATY

States may be induced to accede to a convention if it provides that, at their request, an international agency may carry out functions which, pursuant to that convention, are incumbent upon contracting States.

The Convention on International Civil Aviation, 1944 (also containing the Constitution of the International Civil Aviation Organization), refers to such assistance:

Art. 71. *Provision and maintenance of facilities by (I.C.A.O.) Council.* If a contracting State so requests, the [I.C.A.O.] Council may agree to provide, man, maintain and administer any or all of the airports and other navigation facilities including radio and meteorological services, required in its territory for the safe . . . efficient and economical operation of the international air services of the other contracting States . . .

H. STIPULATION THAT IF A TREATY WOULD NOT ENTER INTO EFFECT, AN INTERNATIONAL ORGAN MIGHT TAKE APPROPRIATE ACTION

A League of Nations convention on narcotic drugs,[113] 1931, stipu-

---

[112] Art. 8, para. 1: "There shall be established a Committee on the Elimination of Racial Discrimination . . . consisting of eighteen experts . . . elected by States Parties from among their nationals. . . ."
Art. 8, para. 2: "The members of the Committee shall be elected by secret ballot from a list of persons nominated by the States Parties. Each State Party may nominate one person from among its own nationals."

[113] Convention for Limiting the Manufacture and Regulating the Distribution of Narcotic Drugs, 1931.

lated that if the twenty-five ratifications or adherences required to make it come into effect was not reached within two years, the matter was to be brought before the Council of the League, which was to take any measures regarding the subject matter it considered necessary under the circumstances. Thereupon, the League's Advisory Committee on Opium "put on an exceptionally vigorous campaign" in favour of the Convention's acceptance; it did enter into force in 1933 and, in fact, received forty-four acceptances by May 1934.[114]

I. Conclusion of Bilateral Agreement Between an International Agency and a Member State, Subsidiary to a Multilateral Treaty not Yet in Force

In the first half of 1968, when the Treaty for the Prohibition of Nuclear Weapons in Latin America (Tlatelolco Treaty) was not yet in force, Mexico, which was a party to it, requested the International Atomic Energy Agency to "apply safeguards, for the purposes of the Treaty, to its nuclear activities." The request was based on article 13 of the Treaty, which says that "each Contracting Party shall negotiate multilateral or bilateral agreements with the I.A.E.A. for the application of its safeguards to its nuclear activities."[115]

The detailed agreement thereupon concluded between the I.A.E.A. and Mexico on 6 September 1968 contains provisions regarding "Undertakings by the Government and the Agency," "Notifications," "Inventory," "Safeguard Procedures," "Non-compliance," "Agency Inspectors," financial arrangements, "Settlement of Disputes" and "Entry into force, amendments and duration." It was the first of the agreements mandatory for all parties to the Tlatelolco Treaty. States eligible to become parties to this regional de-nuclearization treaty but not yet parties to it were thus furnished with a model which might facilitate their decision to join the Treaty.[116]

J. Number of Acceptances Required and Length of Interval Thereafter to Make a Treaty Come into Effect

States negotiating an international treaty have it in their hands to delay or to accelerate its coming into force by stipulating in it (a) a smaller or larger initial minimum number of acceptances and (b) a

---

[114] Wilcox, *op. cit.*, p. 153.

[115] See also preamble to the I.A.E.A.-Mexico Agreement on Application of Safeguards, of 6 September 1968 (I.A.E.A. Doc. INFCIRC/118 of 24 September 1968).

[116] The I.A.E.A.-Mexico agreement may also be of interest to States contemplating adherence to the Treaty on Non-Proliferation of Nuclear Weapons of 12 June 1968, since this general treaty also calls on parties to undertake to accept safeguard controls as set forth in agreements to be concluded with the I.A.E.A.

longer or shorter time interval thereafter to make the treaty enter into force.[117] The first stipulation in particular might affect the degree of priority which Governments allot to consideration of acceptance. There are some indications that if a treaty requires a relatively large number of initial acceptances, some Governments will adopt a "wait and see" attitude. In turn, if the number of required initial acceptances is relatively small, and if there is a short time interval or none at all between the deposit of the last such acceptance and the treaty's entry into force, this could convey a feeling of urgency on the part of the adopting conference, which feeling may then be shared by Governments and give impetus to their consideration of acceptance.

[117] Sometimes, the length of the interval may be in inverse proportion to the initial number of acceptances required to make the instrument enter into force. For example, the I.L.O. Discrimination (Employment and Occupation) Convention adopted on 25 June 1958 required only two initial ratifications (which had been registered by 15 June 1959), but did not enter into force until twelve months thereafter (on 15 June 1960), that is, two years after its adoption. The U.N. Convention on Racial Discrimination, adopted on 21 December 1965, required twenty-seven acceptances but came into effect one month thereafter, on 4 January 1969, or approximately three years and one month after its adoption.

CHAPTER FOUR*

NATIONAL ADMINISTRATIVE MACHINERY

Preliminary administrative work is regularly required before States accept a treaty, or before their competent organs make a decision regarding acceptance. Some aspects of this administrative work may be influenced by differences in the constitutional law and practice of States.[1] But it will generally be necessary for States contemplating adherence to a treaty to have the competent administrative units (ministries, departments, agencies, etc.) examine the nature, scope and implications of the treaty and the effect it would have upon the State's municipal law, previous treaty rights and obligations, political and fiscal policy, etc. If a treaty requires implementing legislation, the drafting of the respective legislative bills often calls for additional administrative inquiry and inter-departmental consultation.

The resulting administrative problems vary from State to State and according to the subject matter of treaties; but there are some administrative problems that, in one form or another, generally confront all States eligible to become parties to United Nations treaties, and there are certain administrative problems that are common to certain categories of those States.

I. DEPARTMENTAL INQUIRIES AND INTER-DEPARTMENTAL CONSULTATIONS

A. Decision to Start the Preliminary Administrative Work

The first pertinent factor is to decide when to start the inquiries into the respective treaty by the government departments concerned. The

* This chapter is based primarily upon information obtained from informal discussions with officials of twenty States. Available documentary information is also referred to.
[1] See chap. five.

decision lies within the sovereign discretion of the State or, more precisely, the organ competent to exercise that discretion. In the case of certain treaties, the question as to which organ is competent to put the procedure of administrative inquiry and consultation into motion may itself raise jurisdictional problems.[2] It should be noted that States members of the I.L.O. are required to endeavour to solve their jurisdictional problems within a specified period of time.[3]

B. THE RANGE OF INQUIRIES

One of the common factors causing delay in the acceptance of treaties has been the protracted administrative work involved in carrying out inquiries into treaties by several government departments. It was pointed out that in many States the views of a relatively large number of government departments, offices and agencies have to be obtained before the instrument is sent to the legislature for approval or, where no legislative approval is required,[4] before it is formally submitted to the cabinet or other competent government body for acceptance. Representatives of States pointed out that elaborate inquiries and consultations have taken place between various departments and agencies on, for example, human rights conventions, treaties on narcotics and other drugs and the Conventions on the law of the sea, 1958. In one State, the interdepartmental consultations on the latter Conventions were so prolonged that it was able to ratify them only after eight years.

Consultations between various departments, it was said, are generally time-consuming. One national official observed that bureaucratic "red tape" usually lengthened the time required for inquiries and consultation. Another official spoke of instances when inaction on the part of a single official in a ministry prolonged the period of consultation. Apart from

[2] In the legal literature, such jurisdictional conflicts are sometimes subdivided into (a) "positive" conflicts about jurisdiction, wherein more than one government agency claims the right to take the initiative, and (b) "negative" conflicts about jurisdiction, wherein the agency or agencies asked to take the initiative disclaim the right to do so, with the effect that no department wishes to deal with the subject matter and none puts the administrative procedures into motion. On the other hand, even in the absence of jurisdictional difficulties, and if no formal decision to postpone consideration of a treaty is made, administrative problems, such as lack of personnel (see below), may cause delay at the very start of the administrative inquiries and inter-departmental consultations.

[3] See chap. three.

[4] Evidence also indicated that in some States, there exist no specific rules that would specify the criteria for selecting the department that must be consulted on treaties before the preparatory administrative phase can be considered complete; and that on occasion not all such departments are being consulted simultaneously or at the earliest feasible time, but additional agencies are asked for their views on a treaty only after others had been seized with its scrutiny.

such delays, progress towards acceptance is sometimes stopped altogether because of the impossibility of reconciling divergent opinions of different departments. Representatives of more than one State pointed to such inter-departmental differences in connexion with the Conventions on the law of the sea and other treaties. In one country, only the retirement of a head of agency permitted the solution of inter-departmental differences.

Sometimes, the acceptance procedure regarding two or more treaties is linked so that if one of them poses problems to some department(s) or interested groups, acceptance of the other treaty or treaties may be postponed thereby. For example, the United States signed the law of the sea Conventions on 15 September 1958, but submitted them to its Senate for advice and consent on 9 September 1959. This relatively brief delay was officially explained as having been caused by one aspect of one of those Conventions.[5]

Some States have consulted other States with which they maintain close relations regarding acceptance of some multilateral treaties adopted under United Nations auspices.

C. DRAFTING OF IMPLEMENTING LEGISLATION

Treaties that require implementing legislation have presented additional administrative problems. In many States, such legislation is not

---

[5] "As set forth in the commentaries accompanying the report of the Secretary of State to the President, the United States would have preferred that the Convention on Fishing and Conservation of the Living Resources of the High Seas include a provision on the conservation principle known as 'abstention.' Agreement could not be reached at the negotiating Conference, however, on either inclusion of a provision in the Convention or approval of a resolution on the subject. It therefore became necessary, at the conclusion of the Conference, for the Department to determine a course of action with respect to this omission which would be acceptable to representatives of the fishing industry in the United States. Consultations and meetings were held with such representatives during the ensuing months, resulting in approval by the fishing industry of a specific understanding regarding abstention to be recommended to the Senate for inclusion in its resolution of advice and consent to ratification of the above-mentioned Convention." (U.S. Congress. Senate. Committee on Foreign Relations, *Conventions on the Law of the Sea, Hearings before the Committee on Executives J, K, L, M, N. 86th Congress, 2nd session*, Washington, 1960, at p. 83.)

The principle of "abstention" implies that if for example a coastal State, or several coastal States by common action, have, on the basis of research, husbandry and fishing rules, limited the catch of fish in the adjacent high seas, fishermen of other States should abstain from fishing therein (see para. A.1 of A/CONF.13/C.3/L.69). The United States ratified the Convention "subject to the understanding that such ratification shall not be construed to impair the applicability of the principle of abstention, as defined in this reference" (ST/LEG/SER.D/1, p. 330).

drafted in the Foreign Office but in the Justice Ministry (Law Ministry).[6] It was pointed out that the latter often examines the terms of treaties more critically than the former, and that this factor has prolonged the time required for inquiries and consultations. In any case, if a treaty warrants implementing legislation, this alone will usually constitute an additional delay in acceptance because of the time required for drafting and, as the case may be, enacting such legislation.[7] For example, whereas the United States on 14 September 1965 gave its consent and advice to ratification of the Vienna Convention on Diplomatic Relations of 1961, it had not, as of 31 December 1968, ratified the Convention, as the necessary implementing legislation has not yet been enacted.[8]

D. Federal States

Representatives of some federal States have emphasized that, regarding certain types of treaties, constitutional law and practice necessitate additional consultations among departments of the federal Government as well as between federal and provincial Governments. The Canadian Department of External Affairs stated in explaining Canada's position concerning the Vienna Convention on Diplomatic Relations (which Canada signed on 5 February 1962 and ratified on 26 May 1966):

> Canadian fulfilment of many of the obligations set out in the articles of the Convention, especially those relating to tax exemp-

---

[6] In the United Kingdom, such legislation is usually drafted by the Office of the Parliamentary Counsel, in consultation with the Foreign Office and Commonwealth Office and/or other appropriate Ministries. In India, drafting of legislation relating to treaties is done by the Ministry of Law, with the collaboration of the Ministry of External Affairs. In Japan, the task is entrusted to a separate Drafting Bureau for all legislation, including the drafting of legislation. In the United Arab Republic, drafting of legislation is carried out by the Conseil d'Etat.

[7] As mentioned in chap. five of this study, some States not requiring legislative approval of treaties still do not adhere to them until implementing legislation, if required, is enacted.

[8] On 6 July 1965, the Legal Adviser to the U.S. Department of State declared, in the U.S. Senate Committee concerned, that ratification of the Convention "makes advisable certain adjustments in U.S. law and practice relating to diplomatic missions and their personnel. Accordingly, the Department of State, in consultation with the Department of Justice and the Treasury Department, has prepared some draft legislation which . . . will shortly be transmitted to Congress . . ." (U.S. Congress. Senate. Committee on Foreign Relations, Subcommittee on the Vienna Convention, *The Vienna Convention on Diplomatic Relations together with the Optional Protocol concerning the Compulsory Settlement of Disputes, Hearing before the Committee on Executive H, 88th Congress, 1st session*, Washington, 1965, pp. 2-3.)

For further reference to United States practice, see chap. five. See also note 12 regarding Australian practice on the above point.

tions, requires the co-operation of the provinces (particularly Ontario and Quebec, within which all the foreign diplomatic missions and residences are, in fact, located). Fortunately as a result of administrative arrangements between the Federal and Provincial authorities . . . close consultation was undertaken with the appropriate provincial authorities to arrange their subsequent co-operation with regard to the Vienna Convention's provisions. Without this mutual acceptance of responsibility, Canada's ratification of this important international document would have been rendered most difficult.[9]

Concerning the Convention on Road Traffic, 1949 (which Canada acceded to on 23 December 1965), it stated:

Since many of the provisions of the Road Traffic Convention fall within the sphere of provincial jurisdiction, before the Canadian Government took final steps to accede to the Convention it sought and obtained assurances from each of the provinces that, if required, they would be prepared to implement these provisions.[10]

Australian parliamentary debates also show that consultations between federal Government and state Governments had to precede acceptance of certain treaties. Answering a parliamentary question on whether Australia proposed to accede to three named United Nations conventions adopted in 1950, 1958 and 1961, Sir Garfield Barwick, Attorney-General, stated on behalf of the Government of Australia:

Final decisions have not yet been reached. Consultations between the authorities in Australia who are directly concerned with the subject matter of the Conventions are still proceeding.[11]

That federal-state consultations have been time-consuming was indicated by the reply given one and a half years later by the Australian Minister for External Affairs to a question about the progress in the consultations on accession to these and other United Nations conventions:

The consultations between the Commonwealth [of Australia] and the states on the Convention on the Recognition and Enforcement

[9] Department of External Affairs, Government of Canada, *External Affairs*, vol. 18 (Aug. 1966), p. 337.

[10] *Ibid.*, vol. 18 (Mar. 1966), p. 140. While acceptance of the Vienna Convention on Diplomatic Relations primarily required co-operation of the provinces of Ontario and Quebec, where foreign diplomats reside, the Road Traffic Convention required implementation by all provinces of Canada. Apparently, the consultations between the federal and provincial departments concerned lasted a long time.

[11] Commonwealth of Australia, *Parliamentary Debates* (Hansard), *House of Representatives*, col. 2196. 7 Nov. 1962. The question referred to the Conventions on the Suppression of Traffic in Persons, 1950; on the Enforcement of Foreign Arbitral Awards, 1958; and on the Reduction of Statelessness, 1961.

of Foreign Arbitral Awards have now been concluded and consideration is being given to Australia's accession to the Convention.[12]

II. MEASURES TO FACILITATE AND EXPEDITE THE ADMINISTRATIVE PROCEDURES

Developing as well as developed countries have encountered administrative problems of the types discussed, although in different ways. While in developing States the absence of specialized departments has precluded or greatly delayed the examinations and evaluation of treaties, in developed States the very number of specialized departments and agencies has lengthened the time needed for administrative inquiries into treaties, and has increased the incidence of divergent opinions. Hence, in both developing and developed countries, the acceptance of treaties is delayed.

In the following, a brief survey is given of measures taken by States to decrease the administrative problems connected with the acceptance of treaties.

A. INITIAL EXAMINATION OF DRAFT TREATIES

Most United Nations treaties are adopted only after considerable preparation. In particular, draft versions of the treaty are submitted to Member Governments for their observations. Representatives of States with comparatively high record of acceptances have pointed out that these drafts are subject to analysis and comment by the competent departments at the earliest possible opportunity. The Ministry of Foreign Affairs of one such State set up two committees, one on international law questions and one on the United Nations, to advise the Government *inter alia* on drafts of "codification" treaties and other multilateral instruments. The treaty division of another Foreign Office has sought advice on draft treaties from experts outside the Government. Such procedures, it was said, facilitate the analysis of the version of the treaty eventually adopted, and have in some instances reduced the time required for inquiries at that stage.

Available information also indicates that if scant attention is paid to United Nations questionnaires concerning contemplated treaties and to draft texts, officials are less familiar with the substance and scope of the treaty when the final text is brought to their attention, so that they may

---

[12] *Ibid.*, p. 1993. 14 May 1964. In the same reply, the Minister stated that "the consultations in relation to the Convention on the Reduction of Statelessness have revealed that several amendments of the Nationality and Citizenship Act would be required if Australia were to consider acceding to the Convention. The implications of this are receiving consideration." As of 31 December 1968, Australia had not acceded to the Convention on either Foreign Arbitral Awards or the Reduction of Statelessness Convention.

have to make the inquiries and studies at that time that could have been made earlier.

B. MACHINERY FOR CO-ORDINATION

1. *Inter-departmental co-ordinating committee for treaties*

Some Governments have set up inter-departmental committees to co-ordinate the views of different departments in regard to specific treaties. Such committees, which usually are of an *ad hoc* character, have proved useful in overcoming differences among government departments on the treaty in question.

2. *Referral to the Cabinet*

In order to prevent prolonged discussions between departments, it is required in some countries to refer all such unresolved differences to the Cabinet (Council of Ministers) for final settlement. Submission to the Cabinet may or may not depend on a prior effort by a co-ordinating committee of the type mentioned above. In any case, the possibility of referral to the Cabinet appears to have prompted departments to try to harmonize their views on the treaty before their controversy goes to the Cabinet.

3. *Standing committee of attorneys-general of federal and state governments*

In Australia, a standing committee composed of the Attorneys-General of the federal Government and the state Governments considers problems which would result from acceptance of treaties affecting federal-state jurisdiction.[13] The procedure has been found helpful in co-ordinating the views of the federal and state agencies concerned.

C. CENTRALIZATION OF THE ADMINISTRATIVE WORK IN A TREATY BUREAU

Another approach consists in concentrating or centralizing the administrative work on treaties in one unit of the foreign ministry.

In the opinion of representatives of States with comparatively high records of acceptance, the existence of such unit has significantly contributed to that record. They note that their foreign ministries have well-established treaty divisions whose function is to centralize the administrative work on treaties and to render advice to the Government on all questions pertaining to the acceptance of treaties. Most of these States have adhered to over 50 percent of the general multilateral treaties adopted under United Nations auspices.

---

[13] See Commonwealth of Australia, *Parliamentary Debates* (Hansard), *House of Representatives,* col. 2197, 7 Nov. 1962.

On the other hand, information collected from States with low records of acceptances discloses that they either do not possess treaty sections in their Foreign Offices or that their administrative machinery is not adequate to cope with the increasing number of multilateral instruments. Some of these States have not adhered to any United Nations convention or to only a few. Representatives of these States have expressed agreement that the lack of a central unit in their foreign ministries responsible for treaty work is one of the factors limiting acceptances.

Evidence indicates that such treaty offices are in a good position to expedite the examination of treaties by other departments concerned, and to act as a mechanism for inter-departmental consultation and co-ordination.

A treaty office is also best able to maintain and keep up to date a register of all treaties concluded under United Nations auspices, and to collect pertinent national and international documentation regarding the evolution of those conventions, including the developments prior to and after their adoption. In particular, evidence indicates that complete, constantly updated and readily available information about signatures, ratifications and accessions of United Nations instruments by other States[14] has stimulated active consideration of acceptances.

Developing as well as developed States have shown increasing interest in establishing a treaty unit or similar administrative office specializing in treaty matters. The growing number of treaties point to the need for such arrangement. Some Governments which recently reorganized their ministerial administrations have established treaty divisions or bureaus in their foreign offices, usually dividing them into two sections, one to deal with bilateral treaties, the other with multilateral treaties. All functions pertaining to multilateral treaties are entrusted to the latter section. Those functions may include: keeping an up to date treaty register; handling questionnaires during the preparatory stages of multilateral treaties; analysing and commenting on drafts of such treaties; keeping abreast of the work of the International Law Commission and of the Sixth Committee of the General Assembly; organizing participation in plenipotentiary conferences and other treaty negotiations; inquiring and consulting with other offices and departments about acceptance questions;

[14] As mentioned in chap. three, the Secretary-General informs all Member States of each new signature, ratification and accession by circular note. It will be useful for the treaty office to record this information immediately and to advise other government offices concerned.

As a simplified substitute for such a national register, some States have adopted the practice of keeping up to date, on the basis of those circular notes, the annual United Nations publication, *Multilateral Treaties in respect of which the Secretary-General Performs Depositary Functions.*

advising the Government on legal questions concerning treaties; and preparing instruments of ratification or accession.[15]

III. PARTICIPATION AT TREATY CONFERENCES

Informal interviews with officials have indicated that if States participated at the treaty conference and thus were able to play a role in the negotiating process, they were in a better position to appreciate the substance, objectives and scope of the treaties; and that this factor has had some effect on the acceptance decision.

It was also pointed out that the selection of the persons representing the State at treaty conferences had some bearing on that State's subsequent attitude toward acceptance. There was general agreement that the chances of acceptance are favourably affected if officials who know the subject matter and the lawyers of the treaty division participate in the treaty conference.[16] One Government sent a team of experts to the conferences on the law of the sea Conventions and thereafter charged them with the task of co-ordinating the preparatory administrative work for the country's acceptance of the Conventions—a procedure that facilitated acceptance.

IV. PERSONNEL REQUIREMENTS

A. EXPERTISE AND TRAINED PERSONNEL

Many developing as well as developed States have encountered difficulties of varying type and degree in regard to the expertise and trained personnel needed for the essential preliminary tasks connected with treaties. A representative of one Western European State noted that in his country, most treaties require implementing legislation, but shortage of legislative draftsmen has unduly delayed the drafting of legislative bills and hence also acceptance of certain United Nations conventions.[17] Another Western European official observed that in his country, lawyers are trained primarily in matters pertaining to bilateral rather than multilateral treaties, and that this factor has sometimes resulted in inadequate appreciation and analysis of multilateral instruments, with consequent delay in their approval.[18]

---

[15] As illustration, see annex VII: Functions of the Section on Treaty Affairs of the U.S. Department of State. See also Department of External Affairs, Government of Canada, *External Affairs,* vol. 19 (Sept. 1967), p. 369, which describes the functions of the Treaty Section of the Canadian Government.

[16] On participation of legislators in the negotiating process, see chap. three.

[17] This State has accepted 34 of the 55 treaties here analysed; 9 signatures are awaiting ratification.

[18] This State has accepted 18 out of the 55 treaties.

Lack of expertise and trained personnel constitutes a far more serious problem, however, for small States and for some developing States, especially those that have recently gained independence. Representatives of two countries that became independent in 1960 mentioned that they have one or two legal officers in their respective foreign ministries who not only have to advise the Government on all questions of international law, but also must attend international conferences abroad, so that they find little time for the detailed analysis of treaties that would be required before acceptance.[19] An official of another "new" State noted that his Government did not lack lawyers, but that a major impediment to acceptance of some economic, commercial and transport treaties has been the lack of experts in these fields.[20] According to representatives of three small States, two in Africa and one in Asia, there are no treaty experts or other lawyers in their foreign ministries; all treaty matters are entrusted to their attorneys-general, whose main responsibilities relate, however, to civil, criminal and other questions of national law. These three countries,[21] like most small States in similar situations, have been able to ratify only a few treaties, whereas small States possessing adequate personnel and expertise have become parties to a comparatively large number of treaties.[22]

B. OTHER PERSONNEL PROBLEMS

Certain other personnel matters have also materially affected the acceptance of conventions. For example, representatives of an African and Middle Eastern State referred to the adverse effect of the transfer of experienced lawyers from the foreign ministry to diplomatic or judicial posts.[23]

The legal adviser to a Latin American Government has pointed out that although his country possesses an adequate number of international lawyers, few are interested in joining the treaty bureau of the foreign ministry because the position of its officials compares unfavorably with those in the diplomatic service. This discrepancy has created a personnel problem in the treaty bureau. The adviser felt that unless the status of the

[19] One of these States has been able to ratify only 2 treaties; the other has become a party to 10 of the 55 treaties, including 7 through succession.

[20] This State has become a party to five treaties, all of which are human rights conventions.

[21] One of them has become a party to two United Nations treaties, the other two to none.

[22] Three small States in Europe, Asia and the Caribbean area have become parties to 20, 10 and 27, respectively, of the 55 treaties.

[23] Transfers of officials who are experts on the subject matters of treaties, or who were involved in the evolution or negotiation of treaties, also caused delays.

bureau's personnel was raised, there was small chance that it would really become a central mechanism for treaty work.[24]

A representative of a federal country observed that the lack of expertise in one of the provincial Governments has at times prolonged the consultations between federal and provincial authorities, thus delaying the acceptance of treaties.

As mentioned, some States have obtained the services of legal experts and advisers under United Nations technical assistance programmes, and the United Nations has organized seminars and training facilities for government officials involved in treaty work.[25] The British Institute of International and Comparative Law, under a grant-in-aid of the United Kingdom Ministry of Commonwealth Affairs (now the Foreign and Commonwealth Office), has for some years been rendering advisory services on legal matters to members of the Commonwealth.[26] Such advisory services have *inter alia* been requested on the subjects of succession to treaties and implementing legislation.

V. TRANSLATION FACILITIES

Since United Nations general multilateral treaties are usually adopted in the five languages of the Organization, States whose national or official language is Chinese, English, French, Russian or Spanish do not face the problem of translation. Seventy-eight of the 132 States eligible to become parties to United Nations treaties belong in this category. All other fifty-four States have to translate the treaties into their official languages. Informal discussions with officials of such States indicate that some have faced an acute shortage of personnel for translation.

A. EXPERIENCE OF SOME EUROPEAN STATES

Representatives of three European States noted that the need for translation has not slowed down the acceptance procedure. Most treaties are translated quickly by the foreign ministry itself, by the ministry concerned or by the translation services of the legislative bureau. Delays have seldom exceeded one or two weeks. Occasionally, States with a common European language have consulted each other on the translation of United Nations treaties. These inter-governmental consultations have proved to be helpful.

---

[24] The country has become a party to 15 and has signed but not ratified another 14 of the 55 United Nations treaties.

[25] See chap. three.

[26] See the *Annual Report of the Director of the British Institute of International and Comparative Law* (London, United Kingdom) for the year 1967-68.

B. EXPERIENCE OF SOME ASIAN STATES

Representatives of Burma, Ceylon, India and Pakistan have stated that their foreign offices do not require translation of United Nations treaties, since English is the working language for treaty affairs. But they have pointed out that when English is replaced by their national languages, translation difficulties may arise.

Some Asian States require translation into their national languages even if their foreign ministries use English as a working language, because treaties must be submitted in the national language to the competent legislative bodies before acceptance. In this regard, a Nepalese official observed that until recently, his country suffered from a scarcity of competent translators. The situation has now changed, but the finding of equivalent terms in the Nepalese language continues to pose problems.[27] A representative of Afghanistan noted that in his country, it is still difficult to find translators for treaties.

C. EXPERIENCE OF SOME AFRICAN STATES

The Arabic-speaking States in Africa as well as Ethiopia and South Africa require translation of treaties into their national or official languages. The other States on the continent do not at present face a problem of translation, as their official business is transacted in English or French. According to a representative of Ethiopia, translation constitutes a delaying factor in acceptance. The situation of the Arabic-speaking States in Africa is similar to that of the Arab States in the Middle East.

D. EXPERIENCE OF SOME ARAB STATES

Representatives of four Arab States referred specifically to translation as a delaying factor in the acceptance of United Nations treaties.[28] Unlike many countries where translations are the responsibility of the ministry of foreign affairs, translations in these countries are usually prepared by the ministry of justice. This seems to have caused delays because of the need for co-ordination with the foreign ministry. In order to avoid delay in the acceptance of the Vienna Convention on Diplomatic Relations, the head of the Legal and Treaties Division in one of these countries translated the text himself. Information indicates that translation problems also exist in other Arabic-speaking States.

[27] Translations of legal texts are apt to create problems also in the case of other languages. Sometimes the line that divides translation from interpretation is hard to draw, and differences over the appropriate translation have occurred between the foreign ministry and other departments of States. On occasion, acceptance of treaties has also been complicated by the fact that States using the same language ascribe a different meaning to certain legal or substantive terms.

[28] These countries have accepted two, five, five and eight United Nations treaties, respectively.

Since 1955, the Arabic Unit in the United Nations Secretariat has been translating all United Nations treaties adopted by the General Assembly and some of the major "codification" treaties adopted at plenipotentiary conferences. Although the foreign offices of the Arab States are provided with these translations as a matter of course, two circumstances have militated against their full usefulness. First, there has generally been a delay of about six months in the translation by the Arabic Unit of treaties adopted by the General Assembly, and longer delay in the case of treaties adopted at plenipotentiary conferences.[29] Secondly, as these translations are not "official," the foreign offices of the Arab countries find it difficult to accept them for purposes of ratification or accession.

A possible solution, some Arab legal advisers have pointed out, consists in the translation of United Nations treaties by the League of Arab States. This would meet the technical and legal requirements of the ministries of justice of the member States, and the translations would be identical in all States. Since the Arab League apparently has translated I.L.O. conventions and recommendations, it might be persuaded to undertake the translation of United Nations instruments. As a basis for this work, the Arab League might use the translations already rendered by the Arabic Unit of the United Nations Secretariat. In the meantime, Arab States might consider consulting with each other and exchanging translations. Such procedures might help those Arab States which face more difficulties in translation than others.

Regarding other States which face translation problems, it may be recalled that the United Nations Office of Public Information, through its Information Centres, has in the past provided assistance in the translation of the Universal Declaration of Human Rights into many languages.[30] The facilities of the Information Centres could be of some use to States encountering translation difficulties.

VI. THE ROLE OF PERMANENT MISSIONS

Members of permanent missions to the United Nations of some States have pointed out that when their mission followed the course of a treaty through the various departments of their countries, there has sometimes been less delay in acceptance. This indicates the possible promotional role of the permanent missions, which are in a good position to impress upon their Governments the effects of adherence to a particular treaty on the Government's foreign policy.

---

[29] For example, the Convention on Consular Relations, 1963, was being translated into Arabic in the summer of 1968.

[30] The Universal Declaration was translated into sixty-five national languages.

CHAPTER FIVE

CONSTITUTIONAL REQUIREMENTS AND LEGISLATIVE PROCEDURES CONCERNING THE CONCLUSION OF TREATIES

I. THE RELEVANCE AND SCOPE OF THE INQUIRY

Treaty ratification (or accession) involves two distinct phases, one consisting of an act (or acts) by the appropriate organ (or organs) of the State on the national plane, and the other consisting of an act by the head of State (and/or other competent national authority) on the international plane. Although these are separate phases[1] carried out on two different planes, each is connected with the other. Since ratification on the international plane is often dependent on action on the constitutional plane, a full comparative study of the impact of the constitutional law, doctrine and practice of States upon their acceptance of treaties would involve inquiry into multiple issues, such as the locus and scope of the treaty-making powers of States, the relative roles of the executive and legislature in the process of ratification of or accession to different types of treaties, the relation of treaties to national law and others. Such examination, to be scientific, would demand collection and analysis of pertinent data country by country and treaty by treaty.

---

[1] Concerning the relation between "international and constitutional ratifications" of a treaty, the International Law Commission observed in its commentary on draft article 11 of the Law of Treaties:

Parliamentary "ratification" or "approval" of a treaty under municipal law is not, of course, unconnected with "ratification" on the international plane, since without it the necessary constitutional authority to perform the international act of ratification may be lacking.

(See *Official Records of the General Assembly, 21st session, Supplement No. 9* (A/6309/Rev.1), p. 30.)

Practical considerations preclude such a comprehensive approach for the present study. What is attempted in this chapter is a general survey, with illustrations, of the different requirements for adherence to treaties prescribed by different types of constitutions. Since these requirements often include legislative approval, and since therefore the legislative procedures for such approval also have bearing on the acceptance of treaties, the chapter also refers to these procedures, with suggestions for prompter action.

II. A SURVEY OF CONSTITUTIONAL PROVISIONS CONCERNING THE CONCLUSION OF TREATIES

A. States in Which the Executive Possesses Full Treaty-making Powers

In the United Kingdom, in other members of the Commonwealth, and in a few other States (altogether in some thirty-three States),[2] treaty-making is regarded as the prerogative of the Crown[3] or alternatively as an executive act,[4] and the decision to ratify (or accede to) treaties is accordingly exercised by the executive branch of the Government. The system of legislative control over the conclusion of treaties, such as obtains in the United States, Latin America and other countries, does not exist in these countries.

However, the exercise of this executive power has in some Commonwealth and other countries been subject to constitutional conventions. For example, it has been the practice in the United Kingdom to lay on the Table of both Houses of Parliament, for a period of three weeks, treaties that have been signed on behalf of the United Kingdom and require ratification. The practice, known as "Ponsonby Rule," was introduced by

---

[2] Australia, Barbados, Botswana, Canada, Ceylon, Cyprus, Gambia, Ghana, Guyana, India, Israel, Jamaica, Jordan, Kenya, Maldive Islands, Malta, Malaysia, Malawi, New Zealand, Nigeria, Pakistan, Saudi Arabia, Singapore, Sierra Leone, South Africa, Sudan, Trinidad and Tobago, Uganda, United Republic of Tanzania, the United Kingdom, Western Samoa, Zambia. The Holy See also falls into this category. In the case of some treaties, Australia and Canada have encountered special problems because of federal-state relations (see below).

[3] J. E. S. Fawcett, *The British Commonwealth in International Law* (London, 1963), p. 57. For Canada, see, for example, "Some Aspects of Canadian Treaty Law and Practice," *External Affairs,* vol. 19 (Sept. 1967), pp. 369-376, at p. 372.

[4] United Nations, *Laws and Practices concerning the Conclusion of Treaties* (New York, 1953), p. 34 (Ceylon), p. 63 (India), p. 70 (Israel), p. 73 (Jordan), p. 96 (Saudi Arabia), p. 105 (South Africa), p. 120 (United Kingdom); see also A. H. Body, "Australian treaty making practice and procedure," in D. P. O'Connell, ed., *International Law in Australia* (Sydney, 1965), pp. 52-64.

the Labour Government in 1924[5] and was originally intended to apply to all treaties. After being discontinued later in that year, it was resumed in 1929, and has since then been generally observed in the case of all important treaties. It provides Parliament with an opportunity to consider the treaties, but has never resulted in undue delay of ratification. Similar practices have been followed in Australia, Canada and South Africa, for example.[6]

Furthermore, in the United Kingdom and other countries following the common law tradition in this regard, Parliament is normally advised of a treaty that calls for implementing legislation. Practice usually demands implementing legislation if the treaty (a) changes or requires

---

[5] The constitutional practice was explained to the House of Commons by Mr. Ponsonby, then the Parliamentary Under-Secretary for Foreign Affairs, in the following words:

It is the intention of His Majesty's Government to lay on the Table of both Houses of Parliament every treaty, when signed, for a period of twenty-one days, after which the treaty will be ratified and published and circulated in the Treaty Series. (See *House of Commons Debates*, vol. 171, col. 2007, 1 April 1924.)

Regarding subsequent developments, see E. Lauterpacht, "The contemporary practice of the United Kingdom in the field of international law—survey and comment," in *International and Comparative Law Quarterly*, vol. 6 (1957), p. 528.

[6] In Australia, the Government of the Commonwealth, prior to proceeding with ratification (or accession) lays the text of the treaty on the Table of both Houses of Parliament for at least twelve sitting days.

In Canada, too, the Government brings to the attention of Parliament the texts of treaties in one way or another. An analysis of Canadian practice indicates that a joint resolution of the Senate and the House of Commons approving the treaty is normally sought prior to ratification (or accession) whenever the instrument involves: (a) military or economic sanction; (b) large expenditures of public funds; (c) political considerations of a far-reaching character; or (d) obligations the performance of which will affect private rights in Canada. ("Some aspects of Canadian treaty law and practice," *op. cit.*, note 3, p. 374.)

In South Africa, "All international agreements are, in accordance with established practice, eventually laid upon the Tables of both Houses of Parliament and Parliament can express its approval or disapproval of any such agreement. Any such approval or disapproval, however, has no effect on the validity of an international agreement entered into by the Government." (United Nations, *op. cit.*, note 4, p. 106.)

See, however, the following statement of India's Prime Minister in the House of the People:

Treaties and agreements are generally public documents and have either been published or are in the process of publication. Since the making of treaties is an executive function, treaties and agreements are generally not laid before Parliament for approval before they are ratified. If implementing legislation is required, copies of the agreement are laid before Parliament. (India, *Lok Sabha Debates*, Series 3, vol. 24, Col. 4837, 16 Dec. 1963.)

changes in domestic law, (b) confers new powers on the executive or (c) imposes financial obligations upon the States.[7]

In some of these countries, ratification will be postponed until after the necessary implementing legislation has been enacted, but this is not a rigid practice. For example, New Zealand waited more than six years and the United Kingdom almost six years after signing the Convention on the Continental Shelf before they ratified it, following enactment of implementing statutes by their legislatures.[8] Australia, on the other hand, ratified this and the other law of the sea Conventions four and a half years prior to the adoption of the Petroleum (Submerged Lands) Act,[9] 1967, which refers to the fact that Australia is a party to the Convention on the Continental Shelf and to the need for further legislative measures applying uniformly to the continental shelf, the seabed and the sub-soil beneath territorial waters. Malaysia acceded to the latter Convention almost six years, South Africa acceded to it almost three months, Malta succeeded to it over three months before they enacted implementing legislation.[10]

The picture also varied in the case of the Vienna Convention on Diplomatic Relations: the United Kingdom ratified it almost three years

[7] See the practice of some members of the Commonwealth and other States, as described in communications from their Governments to the Secretary-General, cited in the United Nations, *op. cit.*, note 4, especially Australia (p. 7), Canada (p. 24) and Israel (p. 72). Regarding Indian practice, the Prime Minister of India declared in his statement in the Lok Sabha (House of the People):

In the case of executory agreements, i.e., where an obligation is undertaken which requires legislative action to be implemented, or where the treaty obligation will affect private rights or existing law, Parliament will adopt the necessary law or amend the existing law in accordance with the Constitutional Procedures. (India, *Lok Sabha Debates, op. cit.*, note 6.)

[8] New Zealand signed the Convention on 29 Oct. 1958 and ratified it on 18 Jan. 1965, after the Continental Shelf Act was passed on 3 Nov. 1964. The United Kingdom signed the Convention on 9 Sept. 1958 and ratified it on 11 May 1964, after the Continental Shelf Act had been enacted on 15 April 1964. But the United Kingdom ratified the three other Conventions, which it also signed on 9 Sept. 1958, on 14 March 1960, as they presumably did not involve the enactment of any legislation.

[9] Australia ratified this and the other three law of the sea Conventions on 14 May 1963; the Petroleum (Submerged Lands) Act was assented to on 22 Nov. 1967.

[10] Malaysia acceded to the Convention on the Continental Shelf and the other law of the sea Conventions on 21 Dec. 1960; its Continental Shelf Act was enacted in 1966. South Africa acceded to all four law of the sea Conventions on 9 Apr. 1963; the South African Act No. 87 of 1963, relating to the Continental Shelf, was enacted on 29 June 1963.

Malta succeeded to the Conventions on the Territorial Sea and the Continental Shelf on 19 May 1966, three months before Malta enacted, on 28 July 1966, its Act No. XXXV of 1966 in respect to the Continental Shelf.

after signing it, on the day its Diplomatic Privileges Act, 1964, entered into force.[11] Ghana also acceded only upon enactment of such legislation.[12] In fact, Australia postponed its accession for over half a year[13] and Malta for over a year[14] after their respective legislation had been assented to. But a number of States, such as India, Jamaica, Pakistan, Trinidad and Tobago and Uganda, ratified or acceded to the Convention before the relevant legislation had been enacted, assented to or come into effect.[15]

B. States in Which Certain Classes of Treaties Require Legislative Approval

The constitutions of many States[16]—Western European, African, Eastern European, Asian and at least one Latin American State—require for certain classes of treaties the approval of the legislature before the executive may ratify or accede to those treaties. The requirement is, in principle, independent of the need for implementing legislation; the respective classes of treaties cannot be ratified or acceded to unless they are approved by the legislature, whether or not they require implementing legislation. If they do, this requires separate action by the legislature.[17]

The requirement of legislative approval not only involves an addi-

---

[11] The United Kingdom signed the Convention on 11 Dec. 1961; the Diplomatic Privileges Act, 1964, came into effect and the United Kingdom ratified the Convention on 1 Sept. 1964.

[12] Ghana signed the Convention on 18 Apr. 1961, enacted the Diplomatic Immunities Act, 1962, and then ratified the Convention on 28 June 1962.

[13] Australia signed the Convention on 30 Mar. 1962 and ratified it on 26 Jan. 1968, after the Diplomatic Privileges and Immunities Act, 1967, had been assented to on 12 May 1967.

[14] Malta's Act No. I of 1966 relating to immunities and privileges of diplomatic and consular representatives was assented to on 11 Jan. 1966; Malta notified succession to the Convention on 7 Mar. 1967.

[15] For example, Jamaica acceded to the Convention on 5 June 1963; the relevant Jamaican legislation was not assented to until 6 July 1964. The analogous dates for Trinidad and Tobago were: accession on 19 Oct. 1965, assent on 16 Nov. 1965. For Uganda: accession on 15 Apr. 1965, assent on 15 May 1965.

[16] For example, Austria, Belgium, Burma, Burundi, Central African Republic, Chad, Czechoslovakia, Congo (B), Congo (D.R.), Denmark, Dahomey, Ethiopia, France, Finland, Gabon, Guatemala, Guinea, Iceland, Italy, Ivory Coast, Jordan, Kuwait, Lebanon, Madagascar, Mali, Mauritania, Morocco, Niger, Norway, Rwanda, Senegal, Syria, Somalia, Sweden, Togo, United Arab Republic, Upper Volta, Yemen.

[17] On the other hand, since legislative approval of the treaty and enactment of implementing legislation are distinct from each other (although the legislature can determine both together), constitutional law and practice may permit legislative approval and, thereupon, ratification or accession, before legislation is passed.

tional organ or organs in determining whether to adhere to the treaty, it also adds a new time element as regards ratification (accession) on the international plane. For, in countries where legislative approval is not required and the executive possesses treaty-making power, the decision about acceptance, as well as the decision about the appropriate time for acceptance, lies in principle with the executive. In countries where legislative approval is required, the executive will probably submit the treaty to the legislature for approval only if and when the executive considers acceptance to be desirable. However, once the treaty is submitted to the legislature, the latter may thereupon, according to the country's constitutional law and practice, determine itself the time at which it wishes to consider the treaty.

Constitutions requiring legislative approval differ from each other as regards the classes of treaties for which this requirement prevails. Some constitutions ask approval for only one or a few types of treaties; others are more exacting. The Belgian Constitution of 1831, which served as a model for a number of European constitutions, provides in article 68:

> Le Roi fait les traités de paix, d'alliance et de commerce. Il en donne connaissance aux Chambres aussitôt que l'intérêt et la sûreté de l'Etat le permettent, en y joignant les communications convenables. Les traités de commerce et coux qui pourraient grever l'Etat ou lier individuellement des Belges n'ont d'effet qu'après avoir reçu l'assentiment des Chambres. . . .

In a memorandum to the Secretary-General of the United Nations of 6 March 1951, the Belgian Government explained the scope of this provision as follows:

> Il résulte des ces dispositions que la conclusion des conventions internationales est une prérogative du pouvoir exécutif, exercée, comme les autres attributions de ce pouvoir, par le Roi sous la responsabilité d'un Ministre. . . . Lorsque l'assentiment des Chambres est requis pour que la convention porte ses effets, la ratification du Chef de l'Etat n'intervient généralement que lorsque cet assentiment est acquis.[18]

The French Constitution of 1958 lists the following types of treaties as requiring legislative approval (article 53):

> Peace treaties, commercial treaties, treaties or agreements relative to international organization, those that imply a commitment for the finances of the State, those that modify provisions of a legislative nature, those relative to the status of persons; those that call for the cession, exchange or addition of territory may be

---

[18] United Nations, *op. cit.*, note 4, pp. 15-16. The Belgian Memorandum, *ibid.*, p. 16 says: "en certains cas urgents la ratification a été donnée avant l'approbation des Chambres." Regarding the interpretation and application of art. 68, see generally, P.F. Smets, *L'Assentiment des Chambres Législatives aux Traités Internationaux* (Bruxelles, 1964).

ratified or approved only by law. They shall go into effect only after having been ratified or approved.[19]

This article incorporates, in essence, article 27 of the Constitution of the Fourth Republic, on which the Government of France commented in a communication to the Secretary-General:

L'intervention du pouvoir législatif quand elle est requise ne l'est qu'à un des derniers stades de la procédure. Le Parlement au moyen d'une loi autorise l'Exécutif à donner une ratification en vertu de laquelle la France sera engagée par le Traité.[20]

The Constitutions of the French-speaking countries in Africa generally contain provisions similar to those of the Constitution of the Fifth Republic as regards the classes of treaties requiring legislative approval.[21] The Constitution of Morocco (article 31) limits parliamentary control to "treaties which imply a commitment for the finances of the State," whereas, for example, the Constitutions of Czechoslovakia,[22] Ethiopia,[23] the Republic of Korea,[24] Somalia[25] and the United Arab Republic[26] require legislative approval prior to ratification or accession for various classes of treaties.

---

[19] For a commentary on art. 53 and related aspects of French treaty law, see, for example, M. Lesage, "Les Procédures de Conclusion des Accords Internationaux de la France sous la Vème République" in *Annuaire Français de Droit International,* vol. 8 (1962), pp. 873-888.

[20] United Nations, *op. cit.,* note 4, p. 49.

[21] See, for example, the Constitutions of Burundi (art. 60); Central African Republic (art. 34); Chad (art. 70); Congo (B.) (art. 61); Congo (D. R.) (art. 9); Dahomey (art. 93); Gabon (art. 52); Guinea (art. 33); Ivory Coast (art. 54); Madagascar (art. 14); Mali (art. 38); Mauritania (art. 44); Niger (art. 54); Rwanda (art. 56); Togo (art. 67); Upper Volta (art. 54).

[22] Art. 42 of the Constitution, 1960: ". . . political and economic treaties of a general character, as well as such treaties as require legislation in order to be carried into effect, shall require approval by the National Assembly prior to ratification . . ." A Constitutional Act of 28 Oct. 1968, which introduced the federal system, amended the provision to the effect that such treaties require approval by the bicameral federal Assembly . . .

[23] Art. 30 of the Constitution, 1955: ". . . all treaties of peace and all treaties or international agreements involving a modification of the territory of the Empire or of a sovereignty or jurisdiction over any part of such territory, or laying a burden on Ethiopian subjects personally, or modifying legislation in existence or requiring expenditure of State funds, or involving loans or monopolies, shall, before becoming binding upon the Empire and inhabitants thereof, be laid before Parliament and if both Houses of Parliament shall approve the same . . . shall then be submitted to the Emperor for ratification."

[24] Art. 56 (1) of the Constitution, 1948: "The National Assembly shall have the right of concurrence to the ratification of treaties pertaining to mutual assistance or mutual security, treaties concerning international organizations, treaties of commerce, fishery, peace, treaties which would cause a financial obligation for the State or its nationals, treaties concerning

The Swedish Constitution of 1812, as amended, requires in article 12 approval by the Riksdag for agreements which deal with matters to be decided under the Constitution by the Riksdag, "either alone or with the King," and in general for agreements that are "of major importance."[27] The Swedish Government, in a memorandum of 28 May 1951, stated that the following classes of treaties fall under these definitions: (a) agreements the execution of which calls for a statute; (b) agreements of major importance, that is, those requiring legislation falling within the King's constitutional power to make administrative law; (c) agreements which do not call for special legislation but may nevertheless impose obligations upon the State, e.g., most political treaties; (d) agreements concerning conciliation, juridical decisions and arbitral awards. The question whether a treaty is of major importance is decided by the King, after consultation with the Council of State.[28]

The Norwegian Constitution of 1814, as amended, contains similar provisions, but instead of referring to treaties of "major importance" as in the Swedish Constitution, it uses the term "special importance."[29] A communication from the Norwegian Government shows that the term has been broadly interpreted: "In spite of the expression 'of special importance,' the rule is to obtain the consent of the Storting regarding all treaties of any importance."[30]

Although in the Scandinavian countries the legislature usually considers specific treaties coming up for approval, there have been cases where the legislature consented in advance to the conclusion of treaties.

---

the status of alien forces in the territory, or treaties related to legislative matters."

[25] Art. 67: "The Assembly authorizes by law the ratification of political, military, and commercial international treaties or of those which involve modifications of laws or financial expenditures not foreseen in the budget."

[26] Art. 125 of the Constitution, 1964: ". . . peace treaties, pacts, commercial and maritime treaties and treaties involving modifications in the territory of the State, or connected with the rights of sovereignty, or which lay upon the Treasury of the State charges not provided for in the budget, shall not be in force unless they are approved by the National Assembly."

[27] Art. 12: "The King shall have power to enter into agreements with foreign Powers after the Council of State has been heard upon the subject. When such agreements deal with matters which are required under this instrument of government to be decided by the Riksdag, either alone or with the King, or when, though not dealing with such matters, they are of major importance, they shall be laid before the Riksdag for approval; and such agreements shall contain a reservation making their validity depending upon the Riksdag's sanction."

[28] United Nations, op. cit., note 4, p. 97 and 98.

[29] See art. 26 of the Norwegian Constitution.

[30] United Nations, op. cit., note 4, p. 91.

C. Legislative Bodies Competent for Approval of Treaties

The constitutional law and practice of States requiring legislative approval prior to ratification or accession differs not only in regard to the classes of treaties for which this procedure is prescribed, but also in regard to the legislative bodies whose approval is required.

1. *States in which the consent of the upper house of the legislature is required*

In some States,[31] prior consent or approval by the upper house of the legislature is necessary for treaty ratification. The best-known example is the Constitution of the United States: article II, section 2, says that the President "shall have Power, by and with the Advice and Consent of the Senate, to make Treaties, provided two-thirds of the Senators present concur. . ." This constitutional principle governs the making of treaties other than "international agreements." Whether a particular instrument is a "treaty" within the meaning of article II, section 2, is, however, a question of domestic constitutional law which cannot be answered by "an inflexible rule of thumb" applicable in all circumstances.[32] The following information, contained in a statement by the United Nations Secretariat which was subsequently approved by the United States Government, lists the classess of "international agreements" other than treaties: (a) agreements or understandings entered into with foreign Governments pursuant to or in accordance with specific directions or authorization by the U.S. Congress; (b) agreements or understandings made with foreign Governments but not given effect except with the approval of the Congress, by specific sanction or implementation; and (3) agreements or understandings made with foreign Governments by the Executive solely under and in accordance with the Executive's constitutional power.[33]

The provisions of the Constitutions of Liberia,[34] Mexico and the Philippines[35] regarding the conclusion of treaties are similar to those of the United States. But while the latter requires concurrence of two thirds of the Senators who are "present" at the respective vote, the Philippine Constitution stipulates that "concurrence of two-thirds of all the members of the Senate" is necessary, so that the number of Senate votes required for concurrence is not decreased if fewer than all Senators are present when the vote is taken. The Mexican Constitution does not explicitly

---

[31] Ecuador, Liberia, Mexico, the Philippines, the United States.

[32] See United Nations, *op. cit.*, note 4, p. 129.

[33] United Nations, *op. cit.*, note 4, p. 130.

[34] Art. 3(1) of the Constitution, 1955.

[35] Art. 4(7) of the Constitution, 1935, as amended.

state the vote necessary for approval of treaties and diplomatic conventions.[36]

2. *States in which the consent of the unicameral legislature is required*

In a number of different countries,[37] the approval of treaties prior to ratification, insofar as required, lies with the unicameral legislature (styled National Assembly, Congress, etc.). Some of the Constitutions in this group, however, are considerably more explicit than others in regulating the relative roles of the legislature and of the executive in the conclusion of treaties. For example, article 46 of the previous Constitution of Cambodia limited itself to stating: "The King shall sign treaties and conventions with foreign States and shall ratify them by vote of the National Assembly"; and article 11 of the Constitution of Indonesia provides: "The President, with the agreement of the DeWan Perwakilan Rajkat [Legislature] . . . concludes treaties with other States."[38] On the other hand, the Constitution of Costa Rica, for example, specifically lists among the exclusive powers of the Legislative Assembly "to approve or disapprove international conventions, public treaties and concordats" and assigns to the President the power to "make agreements, public treaties and concordats, to promulgate and execute them following their approval and ratification by the Legislative Assembly according to the provisions of this Constitution."[39] Similarly elaborate provisions are found in the Constitutions of El Salvador,[40] Haiti,[41] Honduras[42] and Panama.[43] The Haitian Constitution (article 59) adds the requirement of a two-thirds vote of all members of the Legislature for the approval of treaties. The Constitution of Honduras implies a distinction between "treaties" and "agreements" by requiring the President to submit "treaties" to the legislature for "ratifications" (article 201, section 26), but not stipulating such requirement in article 201, section 27, referring to the President's power "to make any other kind of economic or cultural agreement."

---

[36] Art. 76 of the Mexican Constitution, 1917: "The exclusive powers of the Senate are: (1) to approve the treaties and diplomatic conventions concluded by the President of the Republic with the Foreign Powers. . ."

[37] For example, Cambodia, Cameroon, El Salvador, Haiti, Honduras, Indonesia, Iran, Laos, Luxembourg, Panama, Tunisia.

[38] The Constitutions of Cameroon, Iran, Laos, Luxembourg and Tunisia are also less detailed in this respect than are the Constitutions of Latin American countries in this group.

[39] Arts. 121(4) and 140(10) of the Constitution, 1949.

[40] Arts. 47(29) and 78(12) of the Constitution, 1962.

[41] Arts. 56(3) and 93 of the Constitution, 1964.

[42] Arts. 181(26) and 201(26) of the Constitution, 1965.

[43] Arts. 118(5) and 144(8) of the Constitution, 1946.

3. *States in which the consent of the bicameral legislature is required*

In various European and Latin American countries and certain other countries with a bicameral legislature,[44] the consent of both houses is necessary for ratification of or accession to treaties.

As was seen in the case of countries with a unicameral legislature, the constitutional provisions of countries with a bicameral system also vary among each other. Some, especially in Latin America, lay down more explicit and detailed rules than others regarding the relative role of the executive and the legislature in the conclusion of treaties. Thus the Constitution of Brazil, 1947, bestows by article 47(1) on the National Congress (which consists of the Chamber of Deputies and the Federal Senate) the "exclusive power . . . to render final decision regarding the treaties concluded by the President of the Republic," and by article 83(viii) requires the President "to conclude international treaties, conventions, and acts subject to approval by the National Congress."

In Chile, one of the exclusive "attributes" of the Congress (composed of the Chamber of Deputies and the Senate) is to "approve or disapprove treaties," while the President has the "special attribute" to "conclude and sign all treaties of peace, alliance, truce, neutrality, commerce, concordats and other conventions. Treaties before their ratification must be presented for the approval of Congress. . ."[45] Analogous provisions are to be found in several Latin American countries.[46] But

---

[44] For example, Afghanistan, Belgium, Bolivia, Brazil, Chile, Colombia, Czechoslovakia (since the change from a unicameral to a bicameral system late in 1968), Dominican Republic, France, Italy, Nicaragua, Paraguay, Peru, Uruguay, Venezuela. Regarding the Netherlands and Japan, see below.

[45] Arts. 43(5) and 72(16) of the Constitution, 1925. A memorandum of the Permanent Mission of Chile to the United Nations states, however:
> It has been generally understood that a distinction should be drawn between treaties in the strict constitutional sense and international undertakings which, as a group, might be called agreements in a simplified form, requiring no parliamentary approval or ratification. The latter, under the Chilean constitutional system, may refer only to matters within the ordinary competence of the Executive Power and have not the effect, under domestic law, of an Act of Congress. They include administrative agreements, agreements specifying measures of execution, the interpretation of previous conventions and other conventions of a similar type. (United Nations, *op. cit.,* note 4, p. 35.)

[46] See Constitutions of Bolivia, 1967, arts. 59(12) and 96(2); Colombia, 1886, arts. 76(22) and 120(20); Dominican Republic, 1966, arts. 37(14) and 55(6); Paraguay, 1940, arts. 51(11), 63(2) and 76(8); Peru, 1933, arts. 123(21) and 154(20); Uruguay, 1967, arts. 83(7) and 168(20).
However, in Peru
> it has become the practice for such agreements as do not, in any of their articles, modify, alter or derogate from any existing law to be

constitutions of other States providing for bicameral legislative consent are less explicit. For example, the Constitution of Libya, 1961, says that "the King shall declare war and conclude peace and enter into treaties which he ratifies after the approval of Parliament."[47] The formulation in the Constitution of Afghanistan, 1964, reads, "The ratification of international treaties, dispatch abroad of detachments of Afghan armed forces . . . are within the competence of the "Shura.""[48]

D. STATES IN WHICH THE PRESIDIUM OR SIMILAR BODIES RATIFY TREATIES

This type of procedure is to be found in the Constitutions of Albania, the Byelorussian S.S.R., Bulgaria, Hungary, Mongolia, Romania, the Ukrainian S.S.R. and the Union of Soviet Socialist Republics, among others. It can be exemplified by a succinct description of the relevant provisions of the constitutions of two of these countries.

1. *Union of Soviet Socialist Republics*

Pursuant to article 31 of the Constitution.

The [bicameral] Supreme Soviet of the U.S.S.R. exercises all rights vested in the Union of Soviet Socialist Republics in accordance with Article 14[49] of the Constitution, in so far as they do not, by virtue of the Constitution, come within the jurisdiction of organs of the U.S.S.R. that are accountable to the Supreme Soviet of the U.S.S.R., that is, the Presidium of the Supreme Soviet of the U.S.S.R., the Council of Ministers of the U.S.S.R., and the Ministries of the U.S.S.R.

Article 49 describes the functions of the Presidium; in addition to other functions cited there, the Presidium "ratifies and denounces international treaties of the U.S.S.R." Hence, the Presidium of the Supreme Soviet of the U.S.S.R., which is elected at a joint sitting of the two Chambers of the Supreme Soviet, is the organ that ratifies treaties in the U.S.S.R.

---

approved by means of decisions of the Executive Power (*resolución suprema*), since it is within the competence of the Executive Power to enact provisions which, from the juridical point of view, are second only to the laws enacted by the Legislative Power. (United Nations, *op. cit.*, note 4, pp. 93-94.)

[47] Art. 69. The Parliament consists of the Senate and the House of Representatives.

[48] See art. 64. According to art. 42, the Shura (Parliament) consists of the Wolesi Jirgah (House of the People) and the Meshrano Jirgah (House of the Elders).

[49] Art. 14: "The jurisdiction of the Union of Soviet Socialist Republics, as represented by its higher organs of State power and organs of State administration, embraces: (a) Representation of the U.S.S.R. in international relations, conclusion, ratification and denunciation of treaties of the U.S.S.R. with other States, establishment of general procedure governing the relations of the Union Republics with foreign States. . . ."

The Soviet practice shows examples of ratification of treaties by the Supreme Soviet also. For instance, the Supreme Soviet ratified the Treaty of Alliance between the U.S.S.R. and the United Kingdom of 26 May 1942. The ratification is in such cases effected by the Supreme Soviet in its capacity as the supreme organ of State Power in the U.S.S.R., which "is competent to carry out also those functions of the 'Head of State' in the field of international representation and international treaties that the constitution vested in the Presidium."[50]

2. *Hungary*

The Hungarian Constitution entrusts the Presidential Council of the People's Republic with the function of "ratifying international treaties."[51] The Presidential Council is the Hungarian counterpart of the Presidium of the Supreme Soviet of the U.S.S.R. It consists of a President, two Vice-Presidents, a Secretary, and seventeen members, all elected by the unicameral Parliament from among its members.

E. Express or Tacit Approval by the Legislature

The Constitution of the Netherlands of 1815, as amended, provides for tacit ("implicit") approved by the legislature, as an alternative to express ("explicit") approval. The relevant articles regulate the matter as follows.

First, the requirement of approval by the States-General (bicameral legislature) is stipulated:

> Agreements with other Powers and with organizations based on international law shall be concluded by or by authority of the King. If required by such agreements they shall be ratified by the King.
>
> The agreements shall be communicated to the States-General as soon as possible; they shall not be ratified and they shall not enter into force until they have received the approval of the States-General. (art. 60.)

The next article empowers the executive to ask the legislature for implicit approval and lays down the conditions under which implicit approval is thereupon deemed to have been given:

> Implicit approval has been given if, within thirty days after the agreement has been submitted for that purpose to both Chambers of the States-General, no statement has been made by or on behalf of either Chamber or by at least one fifth of the constitutional number of members of either Chamber, expressing the wish that the agreement shall be subject to explicit approval. (art. 61.)

[50] O. E. Polents, *Ratifikatsiya Mezhdhunarodnykh Dogovorov* (Moscow, 1950), p. 34 (in Russian).

[51] See arts. 19(1) and 20(g) of the Constitution, 1949, as amended.

The practice of the Netherlands Government indicates that extensive use has been made of the device of tacit approval of treaties.[52]

A further provision of the Constitution (article 62) excepts four types of international instruments from the requirement of approval, explicit or implicit, by the legislature:

(a) if the agreement is one with respect to which this has been laid down by law;

(b) if the agreement is exclusively concerned with the execution of an approved agreement, provided the Act regulating the approval does not contain any reservations in this respect;

(c) if the agreement does not impose considerable pecuniary obligations on the Kingdom and if it has been concluded for a period not exceeding one year;

(d) if in exceptional cases of a compelling nature it would be decidedly detrimental to the interests of the Kingdom if the agreement were not to enter into force before it has been approved.[53]

F. PRIOR OR SUBSEQUENT APPROVAL BY THE LEGISLATURE

As noted, the Netherlands Government is authorized, in exceptionally urgent situations, to ratify or accede to a treaty requiring legislative approval before such approval has been given, but is subject to the subsequent approval of the legislature.[54]

The possibility of subsequent rather than prior approval of treaties by the legislature is also provided for in the Constitutions of Japan and Venezuela.

Article 65 of the Japanese Constitution of 3 May 1947 vests the executive power in the Cabinet; article 73 adds specifically that the Cabinet has the power to "conclude treaties," but with the proviso that

---

[52] According to one estimate, of the treaties concluded by the Netherlands between 1954 (when the constitutional amendment introducing this system went into effect) and 1961, "the ratio works out three to one in favour of tacit approval."

(Kaye Holloway, *Modern Trends in Treaty Law* (London, 1967), p. 372.)

[53] Art. 62 adds two qualifications to sub-sec. (d):

(1) "An agreement as referred to under (d) shall, however, be submitted for the approval of the States-General without delay. In this case Article 61 applies. [That is, implicit approval can be asked for by the Government and given by the legislature.] If the States-General withhold their approval, the agreement shall be terminated as soon as shall be compatible with the provisions of the agreement."

(2) "An agreement shall not be concluded but subject to the reservation that it shall be terminated if the States-General withhold their approval, provided this should be decidedly detrimental to the interests of the Kingdom."

[54] See art. 62(d) of the Netherlands Constitution, and note 53.

the Cabinet "shall obtain prior or, depending on the circumstances, subsequent approval of the Diet."[55]

In Venezuela, the prerogative of the executive to seek legislative approval of a treaty after it has ratified or acceded to the treaty is in three ways more circumscribed than it is in Japan. The Japanese Constitution assigns the power to seek approval to the executive; the executive may exercise that power "depending on the circumstances"; and the Japanese Constitution does not say that a treaty so ratified may be only provisionally executed until it obtains legislative approval. The Venezuelan Constitution permits the executive to accept a treaty not yet approved by the legislature only on authorization by a legislative committee; that committee may give such authorization only "when urgency so requires"; and the instrument can then be only provisionally executed by Venezuela, until approved or disapproved by the legislature.[56]

III. SPECIAL PROBLEMS OF FEDERAL STATES

Some federal countries have encountered special problems regarding acceptance of certain classes of United Nations treaties, for example, treaties on human rights, labour and educational matters. These difficulties arise partly from the constitutional division of legislative powers between the central (federal) Government and the local (State or provincial) Governments and from the scope of the treaty-making powers of the central Government.

As indicated by the illustrations that follow, the nature and extent of the federal problem and its practical impact depend upon the constitutional law and practice of the respective country. In the case of some federations, the constitution makers have anticipated the federal problem and have endeavoured to avoid it.

[55] The Japanese Diet consists of the House of Representatives and the House of Councillors.

[56] Art. 128 of the Venezuelan Constitution, 1961:
International treaties or conventions concluded by the National Executive must be approved by a special law in order to be valid, unless they concern the execution or completion of pre-existing obligations of the Republic, the application of principles expressly recognized by it, the execution of ordinary acts in international relations, or the exercise of powers which the law expressly bestows on the National Executive. However, the Delegated Committee of Congress may authorize the provisional execution of international treaties or conventions when urgency so requires, and these are to be submitted in all cases to the subsequent approval or disapproval of Congress.
Composition and functions of the Delegated Committee of Congress are regulated in arts. 178-180 of the Constitution of Venezuela.

A. CANADA

The British North America Act declares in regard to the treaty-making powers in Canada:

> Section 132. The Parliament and Government of Canada shall have all powers necessary or proper for performing the obligations of Canada or of any Province thereof, as part of the British Empire, towards Foreign Countries arising under Treaties between the Empire and such Foreign Countries.

This provision of Canada's Constitution, however, as a memorandum of 21 July 1952 from the Government of Canada to the United Nations states, "does not permit the Federal Parliament to implement certain types of treaties without concurrent legislative action on the part of the Canadian Provinces."[57] The memorandum also states:

> Section 91 of the British North America Act gives the Parliament of Canada exclusive jurisdiction to legislate in certain fields, while Section 92 gives the Provinces exclusive jurisdiction to legislate in certain other fields, including property, civil rights and the administration of justice. Should the conclusion of, or accession to, a treaty by the Federal Government require implementation by changing the Provincial Statute Law, the Federal Government cannot effect such change without concurrent legislation on the part of the Provinces, if the subject matter lies wholly or partly within the legislative competence of the Provinces. This difficulty is illustrated by a decision of the Judicial Committee of the Privy Council in the case of *Attorney-General of Canada vs. Attorney-General for Ontario* [1937] (Appeal Cases, p. 326). . . . The Judicial Committee decided in this case that the Parliament of Canada had no power to enact, for the purpose of carrying out international labour conventions, statutes relating to matters within the exclusive legislative competence of the Provinces.[58]

Since this decision, the Canadian Government, before adhering to a treaty that involves matters of provincial legislation, consults with the provincial Governments, with a view of reaching agreement concerning the enactment of the necessary legislation.[59] In order to avoid constitutional difficulties due to the federal problem, Canada acceded on 30

---

[57] United Nations, *op. cit.*, note 4, p. 24. K. C. Wheare, *Federal Government* (Oxford, 2nd ed., 1951), p. 179-180, poses the problem as follows:

> But supposing . . . treaties are made [by the federal government] on subjects which, by the constitution of the federation, are given to the exclusive control of the States or provinces, does not this mean that the general government is, through its use of the treaty power, entering the sphere of the regional legislatures? And does not this reduce the regional field considerably? And unexpectedly?

[58] United Nations, *ibid.*, p. 25.

[59] For references to such consultations, see chap. four.

January 1957 to the Convention on the Political Rights of Women, 1952, with the following reservation:

> Inasmuch as under the Canadian Constitutional system legislative jurisdiction in respect of political rights is divided between the provinces and the Federal Government, the Government of Canada is obliged in acceding to this Convention to make a reservation in respect of rights within the legislative jurisdiction of the provinces.[60]

B. AUSTRALIA

The situation in Australia regarding ratification of or accession to certain types of international conventions was summarized by Sir Kenneth Bailey in 1946 as follows:

> From its inauguration, the Australian Commonwealth has maintained that the right to enter into treaty relations with other Countries rests exclusively in the Federal executive. . . . As to the carrying into effect of treaties by domestic legislation, however, the Federation has, until recently, based its practice on the general view that its power is limited by the Constitutional division of legislative powers between the Commonwealth and the States. The exact extent of this limitation was not admitted or defined. But the Commonwealth's action in respect of many international agreements of an economic or humanitarian character assumed, tacitly or expressly, that in relation to some classes of treaties the Constitution vested not in the Federation but in the States the legislative power necessary to implement them in Australia. The Commonwealth was reluctant to enter into international agreements of this kind unless assured that all the States would take the necessary legislative action.[61]

This description is no less true today than it was in 1946.[62] Referring to Australia's position in respect to I.L.O. conventions, Mr. Starke writes:

> As before the [second world] war, the greatest stumbling block in regard to ratification has remained the problem of bringing the law and practice of all, not merely some of the States, into conformity with the Conventions adopted by the I.L.O.[63]

The observation applies *mutatis mutandis* to United Nations treaties which require implementing legislation in the States of Australia. Debates in the federal Parliament indicate the extent to which the federal-state

[60] United Nations, ST/LEG/SER. D/1, p. 291.

[61] K. H. Bailey, "Australia and the international labour conventions" in *International Labour Review*, vol. 54 (1946), pp. 285-308 at p. 288.

[62] See G. Sawer, "Australian constitutional law in relation to international relations and international law" and J. G. Starke, "Australia and the International Labour Organisation" in *International Law in Australia, op. cit.*, note 4, chaps. II and VI, respectively.

[63] Starke, *op. cit.*, p. 130.

problem affects ratification of certain types of treaties. Referring to the Convention on the Political Rights of Women, 1952, Mr. Barwick, Attorney-General, stated on behalf of the Australian Government in the House of Representatives on 7 November 1962:

> The major difficulties in the way of Australian ratification of the 1952 Convention . . . arise from the statutory provisions of at least some of the Australian legal systems relating to the eligibility of women to hold office in the Public Services after marriage and to serve on juries.[64]

In the same debate, Mr. Barwick said about the International Convention for the Protection of Performers, etc., 1961, adopted under the auspices of UNESCO:

> In many respects, the legislation that would have to be passed before the Commonwealth could adhere to the Convention might have to be passed by the Parliaments of the States. . .[65]

On an earlier occasion, Prime Minister Menzies declared on behalf of the Government in the House of Representatives that:

> the question of Australian accession to the Convention concerning the Nationality of Married Women is under active consideration. While Commonwealth law is in accordance with the provisions of the Convention, further investigations are being made into the position of Australian Territories before a decision can be made on the question of ratification.[66]

Australia acceded to this Convention on 14 March 1961, but by 1968 had not accepted the Convention on the Political Rights of Women.

C. UNITED STATES OF AMERICA

Article VI of the United States Constitution declares that "Treaties made, or which shall be made, under the Authority of the United States, shall be the supreme Law of the Land, and the Judges in every State shall be bound thereby, any Thing in the Constitution or Laws of any States to the Contrary notwithstanding." Although no treaty or part of a treaty has been declared unconstitutional in the United States, it is recognized that treaties are subject to "constitutional limitations." In a recent case, *Reid vs. Covert*,[67] Justice Black of the United States Supreme Court said: "It would be manifestly contrary to the objectives of those who created the Constitution, as well as those who are responsible for the Bill of Rights . . . to construe Article VI as permitting the United States to exercise power under an international agreement without observing

---

[64] Commonwealth of Australia, *Parliamentary Debates* (Hansard), *House of Representatives,* col. 2197, 7 Nov. 1962. Ratification of that Convention by Australia had also been the subject of a Parliamentary question in 1960 (see *ibid.,* 6 Sept. 1960).

[65] *Ibid.,* col. 2197. 7 Nov. 1962.

[66] *Ibid.,* col. 849. 6 Sept. 1960.

[67] 354 U.S. 1 (1957).

constitutional limitations."[68] Justice Black further observed that "no agreement with a foreign nation can confer on the Congress or any other branch of Government [any power] which is free from restraints of the Constitution."[69] Similarly, the American Law Institute in its Restatement of the Law noted that "The United States has the power under the Constitution to make an international agreement if . . . the agreement does not contravene any of the limitations of the Constitution applicable to all powers of the United States."[70] In its commentary on "constitutional limitations," the American Law Institute noted that "limitations as those contained in the Bill of Rights apply to action taken under the grant of power to make international agreements just as to action taken under other grants of governmental power."[71]

Although treaties are the "supreme Law of the Land" under article VI of the Constitution, not all treaties are "self-executing" under United States constitutional law. The distinction between self-executing and non-self-executing treaties was formulated early in the judicial history of the United States by Chief Justice Marshall:

> Our Constitution declares a treaty to be the law of the land. It is, consequently, to be regarded in courts of justice as equivalent to an Act of the Legislature, wherever it operates of itself, without the aid of any legislative provision. But when the terms of the stipulation import a contract—when either of the parties engages to perform a particular act, the treaty addresses itself to the political, not the judicial department; and the Legislature must execute the contract, before it can become a rule for the Court.[72]

Accordingly, treaties which impose obligations intended to be discharged through legislative action, or which fail to provide guidance for executive action, are considered to be non-self-executing. Treaties requiring legislative action are usually not ratified or acceded to by the United States until the necessary legislation is enacted.[73]

---

[68] *Ibid.*, p. 17.

[69] *Ibid.*, p. 16.

[70] American Law Institute, *Restatement of the Law* (Second), *Foreign Relations Law of the United States* (St. Paul, 1965), p. 370.

[71] *Ibid.*, p. 372.

[72] *Foster vs. Neilson*, 2 Pet. 253 (1829), p. 314.

[73] For example, the Message of the President of the United States to the U.S. Senate concerning the Convention on the Recognition and Enforcement of Foreign Arbitral Awards stated:

> Changes in Title 9 (Arbitration) of the United States Code will be required before the United States becomes a party to the Convention. The United States instrument of accession to the Convention will be executed only after the necessary legislation is enacted.

(U.S. Congress. Senate, *Convention on the Recognition and Enforcement of Foreign Arbitral Awards, 90th Congress, 2nd session, Executive E,* p. 1.)

Similarly, ratification of the Vienna Convention on Diplomatic Rela-

The "States rights" question gave rise to controversial discussions in the U.S. Senate and within the legal profession in connexion with the consideration by the Senate of the Conventions on Political Rights of Women and on Abolition of Forced Labour.[74] Those favouring an extensive interpretation of "States rights" argued that the two Conventions concerned matters of a domestic rather than an international character.[75] Conceding that these treaties submitted to the U.S. Senate for its advice and consent were "relatively innocuous," they contended that the treaties opened the door for further United States participation in human rights instruments that might not be so "innocuous." Finally, they maintained that the federal Government, being a government of limited powers, was precluded from regulating large areas of intrastate matters. If the area of intrastate jurisdiction were to be cut down, the way to do it would be through internal legislation rather than multilateral treaties.

On the other hand, it was argued that the denial of human rights and other anti-social conduct are proper subjects of international concern. This view was accepted and acted on long ago by the United States, as shown, for example, in *Missouri vs. Holland*,[76] where the Supreme Court held that a treaty for the protection of migratory birds that fly over Canada and the United States was a proper exercise of the treaty-making power. It was maintained that what applies to the lives of migratory birds applies equally to the lives of human beings. The "wedge" argument was criticized on the ground that it is tantamount to saying that, because legislatures occasionally pass bad laws, they ought to be deprived of the power to legislate. It was pointed out that action should be based upon the treaties under consideration rather than upon the fear of possible future treaties. Finally, it was maintained that whether or not a particular

---

tions was withheld until the "complementing" legislation on the subject was enacted. (*Ibid , Vienna Convention on Diplomatic Relations and Optional Protocol, 89th Congress, 1st session, Ex. Report No. 6*, p. 12.)

By 1968, the United States had not become a party to the Convention on Foreign Arbitral Awards nor to the Vienna Convention on Diplomatic Relations.

[74] For a comprehensive account of the differing views on this question, see *International Lawyer*, vol. I (1966), pp. 589-666; see also *American Bar Association Journal*, vol. 53 (1967), pp. 972-976.

[75] In support, the following dictum from the opinion of the Supreme Court in *Holmes vs Jennison* 14 Pet. 540 (1840) at p. 569 was cited: "The power to make treaties is given by the Constitution in general terms, without any description of the objects intended to be embraced by it; and, consequently, it was designed to include all those subjects, which in the ordinary intercourse of nations had usually been made subjects of negotiation and treaty; and which are consistent with the nature of our institutions, and the distribution of powers between the general and State Governments."

[76] 252 U.S. 416 (1920).

matter is of international concern must be determined by contemporary facts rather than by past conceptions.

D. Union of Soviet Socialist Republics

Under the law of the U.S.S.R., international treaties accepted by the U.S.S.R. apply to the entire territory of the Union and therefore to all constituent Union Republics.

Besides, under a provision (article 18a) inserted into the Constitution of the Union in 1944 and under the corresponding provisions of the Constitutions of the Union Republics,[77] the Union Republics have "the right to enter into direct relations with foreign States and to conclude agreements and exchange diplomatic and consular representatives with them."

There is no evidence to indicate that the U.S.S.R. has encountered the problem of federal-state relations in connexion with the ratification of or accession to United Nations treaties.[78]

E. India

The treaty-making power in India is analogous to that in Canada; that is, it is regarded as an "executive act" within the competence of the Government. However, in India the power to enact implementing legislation lies in the hands of the Union Parliament, in contrast to the situation in other federal countries. Article 253 of the Indian Constitution expressly provides that "Notwithstanding anything in the foregoing provisions of this Chapter,[79] Parliament has power to make any law for the whole or any part of the territory of India for implementing any treaty, agreement or convention with any other country or countries or any decision made at any international conference, association or other body." It may also be noted that in India, the scope of implementing legislation is not limited to subjects within the legislative jurisdiction of the Union Parliament. Thus, the "treaty power" in India is virtually unlimited as regards the subject matter.[80]

---

[77] See, for example, art. 16(a) of the Constitution of the Byelorussian S.S.R. of 20 Dec. 1936, as amended in 1944; also art. 15(b) of the Constitution of the Ukrainian S.S.R. of 30 Jan. 1937, as amended in 1944.

[78] The subject matters for which the Union possesses exclusive jurisdiction are listed in art. 14 of the Constitution of the U.S.S.R. As regards the spheres of education, public health, labour, marriage and the family, art. 14 assigns to the Union the determination of basic principles.

[79] The reference to "this Chapter" means the chapter dealing with the allocation of legislative jurisdiction between the Union Parliament and State Assemblies.

[80] Probably the only limitation is that legislation to give effect to treaties and agreements or decisions cannot violate the fundamental rights contained in part III of the Constitution; under art. 13 of the Constitution, any law which violates the rights guaranteed under part III is void to the extent of repugnancy.

F. MALAYSIA

The Federation of Malaysia has adopted rules which differ only slightly from those of India for overcoming the difficulties of treaty-implementing legislation. The Constitution of Malaysia, 1957, like the Indian Constitution, empowers the federal Parliament to make laws with respect to any matter falling under the jurisdiction of the States ("enumerated in the State list") for the purpose of implementing any treaty, agreement or convention between the Federation and any other country (article 76(1)). But Parliament is subject to two limitations: (a) no law can be made with respect to any matters of Muslim law or custom of the Malays; (b) no bill for a law under article 76(1) can be introduced into either House of Parliament until the Government of any State concerned has been consulted.

IV. FORMS OF LEGISLATIVE APPROVAL OF TREATIES

The foregoing survey of constitutional requirements concerning the conclusion of treaties has demonstrated that, in a substantial number of States, treaties require approval by the legislature before ratification or accession. Even in States where the executive has full treaty-making powers, the executive usually withholds acceptance of treaties requiring implementing legislation until such legislation is enacted.

In view of the essential role of the legislature in the conclusion of treaties, it is appropriate to consider the forms in which legislative bodies approve treaties. In some countries, the constitution itself prescribes the form, for example, by stipulating that the approval has to be given in form of a statute. In many other countries, the form of approval has evolved from constitutional doctrine and practice.

Study of constitutions and informal discussions with national officials indicate that there are at least two distinct procedures governing approval of treaties by legislature: either the normal rules of legislation apply; or a special procedure is needed.

A. APPROVAL GIVEN IN THE FORM OF A STATUTE

In some countries, approval must be given in the form of a law. For example,

> The Belgian practice is constant: an Approving Law (*une loi d'approbation*) is voted by the two Chambers; the Law declares, in most cases in a single Article, that the respective treaty—the text of which is annexed to the Law—shall be in full and complete effect.[81]

---

[81] Paul F. Smets, *L'Assentiment des Chambres Législatives aux Traités Internationaux* (Bruxelles, 1964), p. 39: "La pratique belge est constante: une loi d'approbation est votée par les deux Chambres; elle dispose, le plus souvent en un article unique, que tel traité—dont le texte est annexé—sortira son plein et entier effet."

In Luxembourg, according to a Government memorandum of 20 February 1952,

> Les lois approbatives d'engagements internationaux parcourent la procédure législative normale. L'avant-projet de loi, ensemble avec un exposé des motifs et toute autre documentation pertinente, est élaboré par l'administration publique et soumis par le Gouvernement à l'avis du Conseil d'Etat. Ensuite, le projet de loi, avec l'ensemble des travaux préparatoires à l'inclusion de l'avis du Conseil d'Etat, est déposé par le Gouvernement à la Chambre des Députés, en exécution d'un arrêté de dépôt pris par le Grand-Duc. Le vote du Parlement étant acquis et la procédure législative étant accomplie, la loi approbative est promulguée par le Grand-Duc et publiée au Memorial.[82]

Similarly in the Netherlands, ordinary legislative procedures are applied in the case of explicit approval of treaties by the States-General.[83]

The advantages as well as the inconveniences of legislative approval of treaties in the form of a statute have been commented upon in a communication by the Belgian Government to the Secretary-General:

> Jusqu'à présent, la forme dans laquelle l'assentiment des Chambres a été donné est celle de la procédure législative. Cette forme a l'avantage de ne pas laisser de doute sur le caractère obligatoire, en droit belge, des dispositions d'une convention internationale; elle a, par contre, l'inconvénient de soumettre la mise en vigueur de ces dispositions à une procédure lente et compliquée.[84]

Informal discussions with legal officials of some Latin American States indicate the prevalence of the following procedure. The executive submits a bill expressing the approval by the legislature of the treaty (to which the text of the treaty is annexed) to one of the chambers of the Congress.[85] The latter forwards the bill to its corresponding permanent

---

[82] United Nations, *op. cit.,* note 4, p. 81. The Memorial is the official gazette of Luxembourg.

[83] Michael Ameller, *Parliaments* (London, 2nd ed., 1966), p. 314. Regarding the difference between explicit and implicit legislative approval in the Netherlands, see above.

[84] Communication, dated 6 Mar. 1951, quoted in United Nations, *op. cit.,* note 4, p. 16.

See Paul F. Smets, *Les Traités Internationaux* devant la Section de Législation du Conseil d'Etat (1948-1965) (Bruxelles, 1966), p. 57, regarding the evolution of a Belgian legislative practice to vote on treaties in their entirety rather than to subject each article of the treaty to a separate vote:

> L'assentiment des Chambres à un traité doit-il être global ou peut-il être donné article par article? Cette question a été discutée à plusieurs reprises dans la pratique belge. Mais la solution ne laisse plus aucun doute aujourd'hui: l'assentiment doit être donné globalement, en bloc.

[85] In the few Latin American countries with unicameral legislatures, the process is correspondingly simpler.

committee on foreign relations for consideration. If this committee approves the treaty by the required majority of votes, the committee returns it to the chamber. There the treaty is debated and voted upon in the same way as any other piece of legislation. This constitutes the second reading of the bill seeking approval of the treaty. Afterwards, the bill goes to the other chamber, where the procedure of two readings is repeated. A further procedure would govern the resolution of any differences between the two chambers. After both chambers have adopted the bill approving the treaties, it goes to the President for promulgation. Procedural rules concerning the lapse of bills also affect the fate of treaties. In some countries, if any bill is not passed by both houses of congress in one session, the bill lapses, necessitating the resumption of all phases of the process in the subsequent session.

B. SPECIAL PROCEDURES FOR TREATIES

In some countries with bicameral legislatures, the two houses sit in joint session to consider the approval of treaties. The process starts with the executive submitting to either or both houses a draft resolution expressing approval of the ratification of the treaty. The draft resolution then usually goes to the foreign affairs committee of either or both houses. After receiving the report of the committee (or committees), the legislature, in joint session, debates and votes upon the draft resolution. This procedure differs from the normal procedure governing legislation. It obviates the need for two consecutive procedures as well as the possibility of discord between the two houses.

In the United States, the Senate's advice and consent to a treaty is given in the form of a resolution. Rule XXXVII of the Senate, which details the procedure relating to adoption of such a resolution, reads as follows:[86]

> 1. When a treaty shall be laid before the Senate for ratification, it shall be read a first time; and no motion in respect to it shall be in order, except to refer it to a Committee, to print it in confidence for the use of the Senate, to remove the injunction of secrecy, or to consider it in open executive session. . . .
> When a treaty is reported from a Committee with or without amendment, it shall, unless the Senate unanimously otherwise direct, lie one day for consideration; after which it may be read a second time and considered as in the Committee of the Whole, when it shall be proceeded with by articles, and the amendments reported by the Committee shall be the first acted upon, after which other amendments may be proposed and when through with, the proceedings had as in Committee of the Whole shall be reported to the Senate, when the question shall be, if the treaty be

[86] United States Senate. *Senate Procedure—Precedents and Practices,* Charles L. Watkins and Floyd M. Riddick, eds. (Washington, D.C., 1958), p. 578.

amended, will the Senate concur in the amendments made in Committee of the Whole. And the amendments may be taken separately, or in gross, if no Senator shall object; after which new amendments may be proposed. . . .

The decision thus made shall be reduced to the form of a resolution of ratification, with or without amendments, as the case may be, which shall be proposed on a subsequent day, unless, by unanimous consent, the Senate determines otherwise. . . .

2. Treaties transmitted by the President to the Senate for ratification shall be resumed at the second or any subsequent session of the same Congress at the stage in which they were left at the final adjournment of the session at which they were transmitted; but all proceedings on treaties shall terminate with the Congress, and they shall be resumed at the commencement of the next Congress as if no proceedings had previously been had thereon.

Precedents in regard to the adoption of ratification resolutions indicate that the "procedure of consideration article by article" has been suspended on various occasions by unanimous consent.[87]

V. QUESTIONS IN PARLIAMENT

In countries with a parliamentary form of government, members of the legislature are able to "question" the Government (or individual ministers) about its policies. Questions can be, and are, asked for the purpose of urging adherence to treaties.

The procedure, which originated in the United Kingdom, is also in use in many Commonwealth and other countries.[88] "The purpose of a question," says the leading commentary on the subject, "is to obtain information or press for action."[89] Questions are submitted in writing and are answered either in writing or, if the questioner so wishes,[90] orally during the "question period" of the House. After the oral answer to the original question, three supplementary questions on the same subject are permitted by any member. Hence, the procedure is a significant parliamentary instrument and offers various opportunities to prod the Govern-

[87] *Ibid.*, p. 581.

[88] Michael Ameller, *op. cit.*, note 83, pp. 294-299, lists the following countries: United Kingdom, Australia, Canada, Ceylon, Ghana, India, Ireland, Nigeria, New Zealand, Pakistan, Sierra Leone, Federal Republic of Germany, Belgium, Netherlands, Finland, Libya and France. The procedure has also been adopted, with variations, in: Albania, Bulgaria, Cameroon, Central African Republic, Czechoslovakia, Denmark, Ethiopia, Iceland, Indonesia, Iran, Luxembourg, Norway, Romania, Senegal, Somalia, Turkey, U.A.R. and U.S.S.R. (*ibid.*, p. 298).

[89] Erskine May's treaties on *The Law, Privileges and Proceedings and Usage of Parliament,* Sir Barnett Cocks, ed. (London, 1964), p. 351.

[90] The wish to receive an oral answer is indicated by distinguishing the question with an asterisk. An "asterisked" question will, however, not be answered orally (but published in the Hansard) if the member is not present to ask it, or if it is not reached in time.

ment for action on matters of concern to legislators. Studies on parliamentary procedures indicate that questions "exercise a healthy influence on departmental administration, since they are an effective means of bringing to light individual examples of inefficiency."[91]

The "questions" procedure has been employed by members of Parliament particularly in Australia,[92] Canada and the United Kingdom, for the purpose of urging the Government to adhere to treaties and expediting governmental action in this regard. As illustration, a question asked in the House of Lords on the eve of Human Rights Year and the reply to it are here quoted:

Question by Lord Brockway:

To ask Her Majesty's Government how many of the nineteen Conventions arising from the Universal Declaration of Human Rights they have ratified and signed; and if in view of the inauguration of Human Rights Year on December 10 last, whether they will urgently consider the ratification and signing of the remaining Conventions.

Reply by the Minister of State for Foreign Affairs (Lord Chalfont):

My Lord, I take it that the noble Lord is referring to the Nineteen Conventions listed in United Nations Reference Paper No. 6 of June 1967. Of these the United Kingdom is party to ten. In addition we intend to accede to the Genocide Convention as soon as the necessary domestic legislation has been enacted, and we have signed the Convention on Racial Discrimination. Our position on this instrument as well as on the International Covenants of Human Rights and the Convention on Consent to Marriage is being considered and we hope to announce our decisions during Human Rights Year. The principal obstacle to ratification of the International Labour Organisation Convention on Equal Remuneration and Discrimination in Employment and Occupation is the position regarding equal pay for equal work. Only seven countries have ratified the Convention on the Right of Correction since its adoption in 1952. In view of the terms of this instrument we do not propose to ratify it.[93]

[91] The Lord Campion and D. W. S. Lidderdale, *European Parliamentary Procedure* (London, 1953), p. 33.

[92] For some illustrations, see above.

[93] *Parliamentary Debates* (Hansard), *House of Lords,* vol. 287, col. 1261, 18 Dec. 1967.

CHAPTER SIX

FINAL CLAUSES RELATING TO ACCEPTANCE

United Nations treaties provide for different modes of acceptance in their "final clauses."[1] Some of these clauses are more flexible than others. The flexible clauses put less emphasis on formal requirements, in order to facilitate acceptance of the treaties concerned. A comparison of the acceptance records of treaties indicates that these clauses do have an impact upon the number as well as the tempo of acceptances, and that certain conclusions can be drawn regarding acceptance clauses in future treaties.

I. DIFFERENT MODES OF ACCEPTANCE

The different modes of acceptance can be broadly grouped into (A) the classical forms and (B) simplified procedures.

A. CLASSICAL FORMS OF ACCEPTANCE

1. *Signature followed by ratification, accession permitted only after period*

The classical acceptance clauses of major multilateral treaties can be said to be based on the following model: A conference of plenipotentiaries results in the adoption of the treaty text. At the end of the conference or within a period thereafter,[2] the text (or characteristically, a

---

[1] See *Multilateral Treaties in respect of which the Secretary-General Performs Depositary Functions* (ST/LEG/SER. D/1). See its annex: "Final Clauses," for clauses relating to acceptance, including those referred to in this chapter.

[2] The League of Nations Assembly resolution of 1930, which was designed to obtain wider acceptance of League treaties, visualized that a separate protocol of signature would be opened for any new general convention, and that after a certain period of time, the protocol of signature

separate "Protocol of Signature" or "Final Act") is signed on behalf of States specifically entitled by the treaty to become signatories.

However, signatories do not wish to be bound by the act of signing alone. Hence, the treaty (or the Protocol of Signature or Final Act) stipulates that only by a second step called "ratification"—more precisely, by deposition of a formal instrument notifying such ratification[3]—will signatory States become parties to the treaty, provided that a sufficient number of such ratifications (depositions) will make or has made the treaty enter into force.

Furthermore, a multilateral treaty of this type regularly stipulates that, when it has come into effect after ratification, non-signatories can also become parties to it. The modes of acceptance that are to make them "subsequent parties" are regularly not specified in the treaty but are left to their discretion. The expectation is, of course, that this discretion will be exercised according to their constitutional law and practice.

Such subsequent acceptances are evidently required if the treaty is to be widely applicable. Otherwise, all States not qualifying as signatories, or not availing themselves of the right to sign while the treaty is open for signature, would automatically and forever be excluded from becoming parties. This would be particularly iniquitous for States that come into being or Governments that come into power after the expiration of the signing period.

This classical form of acceptance, then, does not require all States wishing to become parties to go through the two-step procedure of signature followed by ratification. The rigidity of this form of acceptance lies rather in the stipulation that unless a specified number (and sometimes also specified category) of States have completed this two-step procedure, the treaty will not come into force at all, and that even if non-signatories were willing to go through the two-step procedure, they could not do so. Hence, an essential aspect of this classical form of acceptance is the difference in weight it attributes to acceptance (ratification) by signatories and acceptance (in whatever form) by non-signatories. Although the latter acceptances are subsidiary, in the sense that they do not "count" towards the required minimum number of acceptances for the treaty to come into force, they still enable non-signatory States to become parties to treaties.

---

would be "closed." (The League resolution of 1930 is reproduced as annex VI to the present study.) On the other hand, as pointed out in chap. three of this study, the I.L.O. has deliberately avoided signature of conventions ever since the beginning of the League era.

[3] States regularly do not question or scrutinize each other's notification that ratification has occurred. This fact tends to imply that States are entitled to claim that they fulfilled the requirement of "ratification" if they formalized or expressed adherence to the treaty in the manner appropriate under their respective constitutional law and practice.

2. *Modified classical form: signature followed by ratification, but accession or adhesion possible at any time*

Treaties embodying the "modified" classical form of acceptance normally provide for acceptance through signature followed by ratification, or accession. Occasionally, other terms such as adhesion are used instead of accession. This form differs from the classical insofar as both ratifications and accessions (or adhesions) are taken into account for the entry into force of the treaties.

The majority of general multilateral treaties and a few limited multilateral treaties provide for these modified classical forms of acceptance. Most codification treaties of the United Nations era prescribe these forms of acceptance. This can be illustrated by the respective clauses of the Conventions on the law of the sea, and of the Vienna Conventions on Diplomatic and Consular Relations.[4]

---

[4] See, for example, arts. 31-34 of the Convention on the High Seas, 1958, and the identical provisions in the analogous articles of the other Conventions on the law of the sea of 1958:

"Art. 31. This Convention shall, until 31 Oct. 1958, be open for signature. . . ."

"Art. 32. This Convention is subject to ratification. The instruments of ratification shall be deposited. . . ."

"Art. 33. This Convention shall be open for accession by any States belonging to any of the categories mentioned in art. 31. The instruments of accession shall be deposited. . ."

Hence, any State eligible to become a party by the two-step mode of signature-plus-ratification envisaged in arts. 31 and 32 is also eligible to become a party by "accession" envisaged in art. 33, and vice versa.

"Art. 34. This Convention shall come into force on the 30th day following the day of deposit of the 22nd instrument of ratification or accession. . . ."

Equal weight is given to "ratification or accession" also by art. 51 and art. 77 of the Vienna Conventions on Diplomatic and on Consular Relations, respectively.

The acceptance clauses of the Outer Space Treaty of 1966, however, do make certain differences between the "weight" of acceptances by different States, although they do not differentiate between the "weight" of different modes of acceptance.

"Art. 14(1). This Treaty shall be open to all States for signature. Any State which does not sign this Treaty before its entry into force in accordance with para. 3 of this article may accede to it at any time.

(2) This Treaty shall be subject to ratification by signatory States. Instruments of ratification and instruments of accession shall be deposited with . . .

(3) This Treaty shall enter into force upon the deposit of instruments of ratification by 5 Governments including the Governments of [the U.S.S.R., the United Kingdom, the U.S.A.]

(4) For States whose instruments of ratification or accession are deposited subsequent to the entry into force of this Treaty, it shall enter

B. SIMPLIFIED PROCEDURES OF ACCEPTANCE

1. *Treaties subject to ratification or "acceptance" by signatories or Non-signatories*

This type of clause still distinguishes between signatories and non-signatories, insofar as it still presumes that signature needs always to be followed by another formality in order to make the respective State a party, whereas non-signatories can become parties by a single step. The difference from the classical form is that these clauses also give signatory States the choice of ratifying the treaty or "accepting" it in any other manner appropriate under the State's constitution. The International Coffee Agreement, 1962, provides for such a choice.[5]

A variant of this form differs from the classical formulas insofar as it altogether omits specific reference to ratification by signatories. For example, a 1949 UNESCO Agreement says[6] that the treaty is "open to acceptance by the signatory States." This formula cannot, of course, prescribe the mode of acceptance under the constitutional law and practice of different States, and hence cannot do away with the requirement of formal ratification if that law or practice so prescribes. However, by omitting any reference to ratification, the formula does not convey the impression that formal ratification is expected.

2. *The "triple option" clause*

This mode provides, in effect, that States may become parties to the treaty through any of three procedures at their own choice, namely, by (a) signature alone (without reservation as to acceptance), (b) signature subject to acceptance or (c) acceptance without previous signature.

As in the clauses just mentioned, no preference is expressed for a particular procedure, nor do the procedures differ in "weight" or "count" for reaching the minimum number of acceptances required to bring the

---

into force on the date of the deposit of their instruments of ratification or accession."

(Treaty on Principles Governing the Activities of States in the Exploration and Use of Outer Space, including the Moon and other Celestial Bodies. Annex to General Assembly res. 2222 (XXI) of 19 Dec. 1966.) In the resolution, the Assembly "Commends the Treaty" and "Expresses its hope for the wildest possible adherence to this Treaty."

[5] "Art. 63. The Agreement shall be subject to ratification or acceptance by the signatory Governments in accordance with their respective constitutional procedures. . . ."

[6] See art. 10 of the Agreement for Facilitating the International Circulation of Visual and Auditory Materials of an Educational, Scientific and Cultural Character, adopted by UNESCO in 1949.

The Agreement thereupon provides separately for accession by non-signatories.

treaty into force. The difference is that the "triple option" clause specifically envisages full acceptance by the act of signature alone; or, indeed, it expects that States which affix their signatures to the treaty but do not wish to be bound by the signature alone will make a declaration to this effect.

The formula is to be found, for example, in a 1946 Narcotic Drugs Protocol,[7] in some United Nations instruments amending conventions of the pre-United Nations era[8] and in some constituent instruments.[9]

The triple option clause differs from the classical form in several respects. It refers to a larger number of choices, and it enables States to become parties upon signature. Furthermore, by avoiding specific reference to ratification, it excludes any doubt as to whether States may adhere by any constitutional procedures they consider most suitable. Finally, this discretion is underscored by avoiding the terms "ratification" and "accession," which terms, under the law or practice of some States, may require a more formal or time-consuming procedure than other forms of "acceptance." Simplicity and flexibility are thus the salient features of the triple option clause. It is designed to foster the adherence of a maximum number of States with as little delay as possible.

A somewhat more conservative variant of the triple option clause is to be found in many of the "limited" treaties adopted under the auspices of the Economic Commission for Europe (ECE). These treaties provide that States may adhere to them by (a) signature alone, (b) signature followed by ratification (if the signature was made subject to ratification) or (c) accession. Some nineteen ECE treaties dealing with various matters of transport and customs contain such acceptance clauses. Although this mode, like the triple option clause, provides wider choices to

---

[7] Art. 5(2) of the *Protocol Bringing under International Control Drugs Outside the Scope of the Convention of 13 July 1931 for Limiting the Manufacture and Regulating the Distribution of Narcotic Drugs,* as amended on 11 Dec. 1946, stipulates: "Any such State [that is, any State which may adhere to the Protocol pursuant to art. 5(1)] may: (a) sign without reservation as to acceptance; (b) sign subject to acceptance and subsequently accept; or (c) accept."

[8] See, for example, art. 4 of the Protocol amending the International Agreement for the Suppression of White Slave Traffic, 1904, and the International Convention for the Suppression of the White Slave Traffic, 1910.

[9] See, for example, art. 79 of the Constitution of the World Health Organization: "States may become parties to this Constitution by (i) signature without reservation as to approval; (ii) signature subject to approval followed by acceptance; or (iii) acceptance."

It will be noted that this formulation avoids any specific reference to ratification but uses the wider term "approval." The second alternative does not envisage a three-step procedure (first, signature; second, approval; third, acceptance) but intends to convey that the "approval" can be expressed by any form of "acceptance."

States, it is closer to the classical form insofar as it refers specifically to ratification. It differs importantly, however, from the classical form in that it enables States to adhere to the treaty upon signature alone.[10]

3. *Acceptance through signature or signature plus ratification*

Another type of acceptance clause also stands midway between the classical form and the triple option clause. This form visualises only two alternatives for acceptance: (a) signature alone, with no time limit, or (b) signature followed by ratification where required by the constitution. Hence it stipulates that once a State has signed the treaty, a further step, namely ratification, will be required only by a State's own constitution and not by the treaty itself. The clause is used in the optional protocol regarding settlement of disputes arising in connexion with any Convention on the law of the sea, 1958.[11]

4. *Acceptance through accession*

A few general multilateral treaties provide for acceptance through accession only. Signature is altogether dispensed with in the "final" clauses of these treaties. Of the treaties examined in this study, the Revised General Act for the Pacific Settlement of Disputes, 1949, the Convention on the Declaration of Death of Missing Persons, 1950, and the Protocol Relating to the Status of Refugees, 1967, prescribe this mode. Some other general multilateral treaties also contain it.[12]

II. CORRELATION BETWEEN DIFFERENT MODES OF ACCEPTANCE AND EXTENT OF ADHERENCE

The possible correlation between different acceptance clauses and the attitude of States towards the respective treaties, and whether, in particular, simplified modes of acceptance tend to improve the chances for acceptance, will now be examined. Since the mode of acceptance is only one among several factors which may influence States positively or

---

[10] See, for example, art. 5 of the Convention on the Taxation of Road Vehicles for Private Use in International Traffic, 1956. States may become contracting parties to this Convention: "(a) by signing it; (b) by ratifying it after signing it subject to ratification; (c) by acceding to it."

[11] See art. 5 of the Optional Protocol of Signature Concerning the Compulsory Settlement of Disputes, 1958.

It will be noted, however, that the two analogous Optional Protocols concerning the Compulsory Settlement of Disputes adopted in connexion with the Vienna Conventions on Diplomatic Relations, 1961, and on Consular Relations, 1963, reverted to the modified classical form of acceptance. These two instruments are acceptable either by signature followed by ratification, or by accession.

[12] Among other important treaties containing this mode, the Convention on the Privileges and Immunities of the United Nations, 1946, may be mentioned.

negatively, the correlation cannot be posited in absolute terms. But while the behaviour of States regarding treaties is obviously affected by a variety of factors, the evidence seems to indicate that the manner in which a treaty can be adhered to may constitute an important factor in facilitating, delaying or preventing acceptance.

In particular, the possibility of adhering to a treaty by signature alone can evidently save the time and effort required for ratification. The question is whether States wish to avail themselves of this simplified mode of acceptance.

A. OPTIONAL PROTOCOLS CONCERNING THE COMPULSORY SETTLEMENT OF DISPUTES

Three such protocols lend themselves well to examination because their substantive provisions are very similar, whereas their modes of acceptance differ. The 1958 Protocol on the law of the sea Conventions provides for simplified acceptance; the 1961 and 1963 Protocols on the Vienna Conventions on Diplomatic and Consular Relations prescribe the classical form.

Of the 38 signatory States to the 1958 Protocol, only 11 States subjected their signatures to ratification; of these 11 States, only 6 had ratified by the end of 1968. In addition, one State succeeded.

The 1961 Protocol on the Vienna Convention on Diplomatic Relations had been signed by 31 States as of 31 December 1968; only 18 of them ratified it. Furthermore the Protocol was acceded to by 14 States, and one State succeeded to it. Thus, 33 States had become parties to it as of that date, that is, during a period of somewhat over 7 years. Of those, only two became parties during 1962, and none during 1961.

Of the 38 States that signed the 1963 Protocol on the Vienna Convention on Consular Relations during the period to 31 December 1968, only 7 ratified it. In addition, 4 acceded to it, so that the Protocol came into force for 11 States during a period of somewhat over 5 years.

The possible advantages of simplified modes of acceptance can be perceived from the acceptance records of two States. The United Kingdom signed the 1958 Protocol on 9 September 1958 and, having chosen to forego ratification, automatically became a party to the Protocol on the day it ratified one of the law of the sea Conventions, the Convention on the Territorial Sea, on 14 March 1960. The United Kingdom signed the Protocol on Diplomatic Relations on 11 December 1961, but ratified it only on 1 September 1964. The United Kingdom signed the 1963 Protocol on Consular Relations on 27 March 1964, but had not ratified it by the end of 1968. France signed the 1958 Protocol on law of the sea on 30 October 1958 and, having chosen to forego ratification, automatically became a party to it by acceding to the Convention on the Continental Shelf on 14 June 1965. France signed the 1961 Protocol on Diplomatic

Relations on 30 March 1962 and the 1963 Protocol on Consular Relations on 24 April 1963, but had ratified neither by the end of 1968.

B. Treaties on Narcotic Drugs

The Protocol of 19 November 1948, which considerably widened international narcotics control, contains the triple option clause. Two subsequent instruments pursuing the same aim, and of which the second is particularly ambitious, provide for the modified classical form of acceptance.[13]

The Protocol of 19 November 1948 has been accepted by 80 States. Nineteen of them became parties upon signature: 14 immediately during 1948, 4 in 1949 and one in 1955. Of the 41 States that subjected their signatures to subsequent "acceptance," none took that second step in 1948; 5 in 1949; 6 during 1950-1951; and as of 31 December 1968, twenty years later, a total of only 27 of those 41 States had taken the second step. However, because 18 States became parties to it in 1948-1949 upon signature alone and 5 "accepted" it under the "acceptance" clause (that is, without signature-plus-ratification), the Treaty entered into force as early as 1 December 1949, one year after its adoption.

In contrast, the Protocol of 23 June 1953, which provides for the classical form, took nearly ten years to gather the number of adherences required to come into effect (8 March 1963). Also, in marked contrast to the 1948 Treaty, no State became a party to the 1953 Treaty within the first six months after its adoption and only 9 during the following twelve months. By the end of 1968, fifteen and a half years after adoption, the 1953 Protocol was in force for only 50 States.

The Single Convention of Narcotic Drugs of 30 March 1961 (the result of nine years of effort), which also prescribes the modified classical form of acceptance, fared somewhat better than the 1953 Protocol but much less well than the 1948 Protocol with its simplifying triple option clause.

The Single Convention received 5 ratifications after signature and 8 "accessions" during the first twenty-one months after its adoption.[14] It took more than three and a half years for the Convention to enter into force (13 December 1964). By the end of 1968, seven and a half years after its adoption, only 41 of the 64 States that signed it had taken the

---

[13] See art. 5 of the Protocol Bringing Under International Control Drugs Outside the Scope of the Convention of 13 July 1931 for Limiting the Manufacture and Regulating the Distribution of Narcotic Drugs, as amended by the Protocol of 19 Nov. 1948; arts. 16-18 of the Protocol for Limiting and Regulating the Cultivation of the Poppy Plant, 23 June 1953; and art. 40 of the Single Convention on Narcotic Drugs, 1961.

[14] Namely, 2 ratifications and 1 "accession" during the remaining nine months of 1961, and 3 ratifications and 7 "accessions" during 1962.

second step of ratification, while 23 had not been able to do so. In addition, 25 States had acceded to it, so that the Single Convention, 1961, was in force for a total of 66 States.

To give another example: the United Kingdom became a party to the 1948 Protocol upon signature on 19 November 1948, the day of its adoption, because the Protocol permits States to become parties by signature alone. The United Kingdom signed the 1953 Protocol also on the day of adoption (23 June 1953). However, to become a party to it, the United Kingdom would have had to ratify it, which it was unable to do during the subsequent fifteen and a half years. On the other hand, it ratified the Single Convention, 1961 (which it also signed at the end of the treaty conference on 30 March 1961) three and a half years later, on 30 September 1964.

C. ECE TREATIES ON TRANSPORT AND COMMUNICATION

The Convention on the Taxation of Road Vehicles for Private Use in International Traffic, 1956, enables States to become parties upon signature; the Convention on the Contract for the International Carriage of Goods (CMR), of the same year, requires signatories to ratify. Eighteen States have become parties to the former treaty, while the latter has been ratified or acceded to by only eleven. The former entered into force within three years (18 August 1959), the latter within only five years (2 July 1961).[15] Whereas one State became a party to the former treaty on the day of its adoption, the earliest ratification of the CMR was not deposited until 22 October 1958.

The acceptance record of another ECE Treaty, the Declaration on the Construction of Main International Traffic Arteries, with Annexes, 1950, also seems to indicate the relative advantages of simplified acceptance procedures for treaties of a technical nature. Like many other ECE treaties, it enables States to become parties upon signature. Of the 22 States parties to it, 4 took advantage of this mode, namely, France, Luxembourg, the Netherlands and the United Kingdom.

Countries whose constitutions differ considerably from each other, including Bulgaria, Denmark, Finland, France, Luxembourg, the Netherlands, Norway, Sweden, the United Kingdom and Yugoslavia, have become parties to one or the other of the ECE treaties upon signature.

D. TREATIES CONCERNING REFUGEES

The Convention on Refugees of 25 July 1951 provides for the classical form. A few States signed it soon after its adoption, but seventeen months later, at the end of 1952, only one of them (Denmark) had followed through with ratification, the required second step. On the

---

[15] The Road Vehicles Convention required 5 States to become parties in order to enter into force; the CMR, 5 States.

other hand, the Refugees Protocol, which updated and broadened the 1951 Convention (Protocol Relating to the Status of Refugees) and which contains a flexible acceptance clause, was acceded to by 9 States within a year, namely, between 16 December 1967, when it was approved ("taken note of") by the General Assembly and 31 December 1967. One year later, 28 States were parties to it.[16]

E. UNITED NATIONS PROTOCOLS AMENDING PRE-UNITED NATIONS CONVENTIONS

United Nations treaties amending certain pre-Second World War conventions on narcotic drugs, traffic in persons, slavery, obscene publications and economic statistics prescribe simplified procedures of acceptance.[17]

The earliest acceptance clause of the triple option type seems to appear in a treaty of 11 December 1946, amending pre-Second World War narcotic drug treaties.[18] Within twenty days of its adoption (by 31 December 1946), 25 States had become parties to it, upon signature, without ratification. Twenty-five States constituted approximately one half of the membership of the United Nations at the time. Hence, that acceptance record would be equivalent to 60 Members becoming parties at present.

It could be objected that the 1946 Narcotic Drugs Protocol dealt with non-controversial formalistic matters. On the other hand, those matters were important if international control of narcotic drugs was to be carried out by the United Nations. In any case, that example also shows that the impetus for quick acceptance may slow down. One half of the then United Nations membership accepted that instrument upon signature within three weeks, but only 5 additional Members did so thereafter. Eventually, 25 other States subjected their signature to "approval"; and

---

[16] The promotional activities of the UNHCR are also a contributing factor. See chap. three.

[17] The fact that these procedures were designed to expedite acceptances, especially by obviating the need for ratification, was explained two decades ago by Mr. Kerno, then Assistant Secretary-General in charge of the Legal Department of the United Nations Secretariat: "The process of ratification had necessarily involved delays. In order to speed up the coming into force of the Conventions, the League of Nations itself had suggested a quicker process, which would enable States, if their Constitutions so allowed, to become parties to Conventions without the need for ratification." *Official Records of the General Assembly, 3rd session, 6th Committee, 90th meeting.* For the League of Nations recommendations alluded to by Mr. Kerno, see annex VI of the present study.

[18] Protocol of 11 Dec. 1946 amending the Agreements, Conventions and Protocols on Narcotic Drugs, concluded during the period of 1912 through 1936. See its art. VII.

of those, 18 subsequently notified approval. Altogether, as United Nations membership gradually increased, 58 States became parties to the instrument.

Another illustration of a United Nations treaty adopted for a similar purpose and containing a simplified acceptance clause is the Protocol amending two pre-First World War conventions against the traffic in persons.[19] Eleven United Nations Members became parties to it upon signature, some even before the end of 1948, some in 1949. Altogether, 29 States eventually adhered to it.

The 1946 Narcotics Drugs Protocol stipulates that the Protocol shall come into force in respect of each party on the date of acceptance, and hence regardless of the number and date of acceptances. This was probably designed not so much to facilitate wider acceptance by States as to make it possible for those provisions which assigned tasks to the United Nations to become at once operative.

*   *   *   *   *

The foregoing survey indicates that codification treaties and major conventions on human rights and on other general topics have tended to employ the classical form of acceptance in its modified version.

The use of simplified and flexible procedures has increased, and the respective final clauses themselves differ from each other in some not unimportant details. Those simplified clauses have until now been inserted into treaties only on such matters as narcotics, commodities, educational matters, or into treaties of a regional type. As demonstrated earlier, various States, sometimes as many as twenty, have made use of one or the other of the simplified procedures. For that group of treaties, acceptance statistics seem to suggest that the simplified acceptance clauses have facilitated speedier and wider acceptance. As a result, most of those treaties have come into force earlier than treaties on the same subjects employing the classical acceptance clauses.

III. TREND TOWARDS INCREASED FLEXIBILITY OF ACCEPTANCE PROCEDURES

In the present era of international relations, various circumstances combine to require an ever-increasing number and variety of arrangements between States. This alone has made it advisable if not imperative to simplify when appropriate the acceptance modalities, especially of bilateral agreements but also of some multilateral agreements without

---

[19] Protocol of 4 May 1949 amending the International Agreement for the Suppression of the White Slave Traffic, 1904, and the International Convention for the Suppression of the White Slave Traffic, 1910. See art. 4 of the Protocol.

legislative ratification,[20] and to make increasing use of the device of "exchanges of notes"—the least formal of acceptance procedures.[21]

On the other hand, although general multilateral treaties of major import are adopted only after painstaking and elaborate preparations,[22] even States that voted for their adoption at the final treaty conference seem not prepared to become bound by them without the opportunity for further reflection inherent in the requirement of ratification.[23] But the trend seems to be that, in general, the decision as to whether or not formal ratification is required should be left to the discretion of States and not necessarily be imposed upon all potential parties by the treaty itself. In other words, the requirement of ratification can but need not be written into the convention itself; and if such requirement is not written into it, the convention may still permit individual States to accept it only subject their own constitutional requirements, such as ratification.

The trend towards flexibility of acceptance procedures, including acceptance by signature alone, is shown in the formulations arrived at by

---

[20] The matter received the attention of jurists even before the Second World War; see, for example, G. G. Fitzmaurice, "Do treaties need ratification?" in the *British Year Book of International Law,* vol. 15 (1934), pp. 113-137. For an account of more recent British practice regarding treaties which are not subject to ratification, see McNair, *The Law of Treaties* (Oxford, 1961), p. 137.

In the United States, "agreements in simplified form" are known as "Executive Agreements." For an account of such agreements, and the types of transactions for which they may be employed, see United Nations, *Laws and Practices Concerning the Conclusion of Treaties* (1953), pp. 125-134.

Regarding "agreements in simplified form" entered into by France, see, for example, Claude Chayet, "Les Accords en Forme Simplifiée," in *Annuaire Français de Droit International,* Vol. 3 (1957), pp. 3-13. According to that study, 30 percent of the *engagements* undertaken by France by the mid-1950's were in simplified form.

Altogether, an analysis of international instruments published in the League of Nations Treaty Series and of some 1,300 international instruments published in the first 79 volumes (1946-1951) of the United Nations Treaty Series concluded that while 53 percent of the League treaties "were ratified" this was true of only 23 percent of the United Nations series. H. Blix, "The requirement of ratification," the *British Year Book of International Law,* Vol. 30 (1953), pp. 352-380.

[21] Of the first 1,000 instruments registered with the Secretariat of the United Nations, no fewer than 272, or 27 percent, consisted of exchanges of note. J. L. Weinstein, "Exchanges of notes," the *British Year Book of International Law,* vol. 29 (1952), pp. 205-226.

[22] As experience shows, these preparatory stages usually last for several years. Their main purposes are (a) to enable Governments to study and make known their views on the subject matters, and (b) to co-ordinate their views even before the treaty conference convenes.

[23] Most of the legal advisors consulted felt that for major treaties, the requirement of ratification should prevail.

the Vienna Convention on the Law of Treaties, 1969. Article 11 of the Convention says that States may become parties to a treaty, *inter alia,* by signature alone or by ratification. This will depend not only on the acceptance clauses of the respective treaties, but also on the ascertainable intention of the negotiating States, as expressed in the credentials of their representatives or in statements made during the negotiation.[24]

[24] The Vienna Convention on the Law of Treaties envisaged three circumstances under which individual States would become parties to a treaty by signature alone:

Art. 12. "The consent of a State to be bound by a treaty is expressed by the signature of its representative when

(a) the treaty provides that signature [alone] shall have that effect;

(b) it is otherwise established that the negotiating States were agreed that signature [alone] should have that effect;

(c) the intention of the State to give that effect to the signature appears from the full powers of its representative or was expressed during the negotiation . . ."

Furthermore, the Convention envisaged four circumstances under which individual States would become parties to a treaty by ratification:

Art. 14(1). "The consent of a State to be bound by a treaty is expressed by ratification when

(a) the treaty provides for such consent to be expressed by means of ratification;

(b) it is otherwise established that the negotiating States were agreed that ratification was required;

(c) the representative of the State has signed the treaty subject to ratification; or

(d) the intention of the State to sign the treaty subject to ratification appears from the full powers of its representative or was expressed during the negotiation."

CHAPTER SEVEN

SUCCESSION OR ACCESSION BY NEW STATES TO MULTILATERAL TREATIES PREVIOUSLY EXTENDED TO DEPENDENT TERRITORIES[*]

The rise of independence and statehood since 1945 of a large number of territories has accentuated the problem of succession to multilateral treaties previously extended to dependent territories. Specifically, three questions have arisen: first, what has been the extent of succession, or accession, by the "new" States to "old" treaties; second, what factors delay or prevent succession or accession to "old" treaties by "new" States; and finally, what measures have been taken on the national and international levels to facilitate speedier and wider succession or accession?

I. THE PROBLEM OF SUCCESSION AND UNITED NATIONS PRACTICE

The problem of succession to old treaties has confronted more than fifty States that have become independent since 1945; and of the fifty-five general multilateral treaties on which this study focuses, approximately fifty have been affected by this problem.

Some of these multilateral treaties had been extended to the dependent territories through a "colonial" clause. According to United Nations practice, treaties not containing such clauses apply in principle to the dependent territories of the parties.[1]

---

[*] Succession arising from decolonization is only one of several forms of succession; it can also be the result of merger and dismemberment of States. The latter are not examined in this chapter.

[1] See the Statement by the Legal Counsel at the 11th meeting of the Third Committee of the General Assembly on 2 Nov. 1966, printed in *United Nations Juridical Year Book* (1966), p. 240.

Under what conditions does the United Nations consider new states to be parties to the old treaties that had been extended to their territories by the predecessor Governments?

The United Nations has applied the following procedures for succession to multilateral treaties for which the Secretary-General performs depositary functions.[2] First, the Secretary-General notifies the new State of the multilateral treaties that were previously extended to it and inquires whether it considers itself bound by them. The inquiry varies according to whether an agreement of devolution of treaty rights and obligations was concluded between the predecessor State and the new State. If there is such agreement, the Secretary-General's letter to the new State says:

> It is the understanding of the Secretary-General, based on the provisions of the above mentioned (devolution) agreement, that your Government recognizes itself bound, as from (the date of independence) by all international instruments which had been made applicable to (the new State) by (its predecessor) and in respect of which the Secretary-General acts as depositary. The Secretary-General would appreciate it if you would confirm this understanding so that in the exercise of his depositary functions he can notify all interested States accordingly.[3]

If, however, there is no devolution agreement nor any other provision regarding devolution of treaty rights and obligations in effect in the new State, the letter refers to the treaties extended by the predecessor Government to the new State during its dependence and advises it of the practice which had developed regarding succession to multilateral treaties:

> Under this practice, the new States generally acknowledge themselves to be bound by such treaties through a formal notification addressed to the Secretary-General by the Head of the State or Government or by the Minister of Foreign Affairs. The effect of such notification which the Secretary-General, in the exercise of his depositary functions, communicates to all interested States, is to consider the new State as a party in its own name to the treaty concerned as of the date of independence, thus preserving the continuity of the application of the treaty in its territory. . .[4]

It is only after the new States have informed the Secretary-General of succession that they are listed in the United Nations publication *Multilateral Treaties in respect of which the Secretary-General Performs Depositary Functions* as parties to the respective treaties from the date of their independence.

---

[2] See U.N. Doc. A/CN.4/150, printed in *Yearbook of the International Law Commission* (1962), vol. II, pp. 106-131.

[3] *Ibid.*, p. 122.

[4] *Ibid.*, p. 122.

Some States have not notified succession; some have notified succession only in respect of certain treaties; and some have chosen to accede rather than succeed, but only to certain of the old treaties that have previously been extended to their territory. Hence, the full extent of territorial application of multilateral treaties has been impaired. In the following, the extent of non-succession or non-accession of certain treaties will be reviewed.[5]

II. THE EXTENT OF NON-SUCCESSION OR NON-ACCESSION

A. Vienna Convention on Diplomatic Relations and the Optional Protocol Concerning the Compulsory Settlement of Disputes, 1961

The Vienna Convention received eighty-two acceptances and the Optional Protocol thirty-three acceptances; two of the former and one of the latter constituted notifications of succession.

The United Kingdom ratified both instruments on 1 September 1964. Since neither of them contains a colonial clause, both would automatically apply to dependent territories. Nine of the dependent territories had become independent[6] as of 31 December 1967: two of them (Barbados and Malta) notified succession to the Vienna Convention and one of them (Malta) to the Optional Protocol. The others have notified neither succession nor accession to these treaties.

B. Conventions on the Law of the Sea

The Conventions on the Territorial Sea, the High Seas, Fishing and the Continental Shelf have received 36, 43, 27 and 39 acceptances, of which 5, 4, 4 and 1 constituted notifications of successions, respectively. All of these successions were by States that had been dependencies of the United Kingdom.

The United Kingdom ratified three of the law of the sea Conventions on the Territorial Sea, the High Seas, Fishing on 14 March 1960. As these Conventions do not contain a colonial clause, they also become automatically applicable to the dependent territories. Of the twenty dependent territories that became independent as of 31 December 1968,[7]

---

[5] Treaties concluded since 1963, such as treaties on Consular Relations, on Racial Discrimination and on the Transit Trade of Landlocked States have not so far been accepted by the major States responsible for territorial application. Consequently, no problem of succession by newly independent States has arisen, and these treaties are not included in the survey.

[6] Barbados, Botswana, Gambia, Guyana, Lesotho, Maldive Islands, Malta, Southern Yemen, Zambia.

[7] Barbados, Botswana, Gambia, Guyana, Jamaica, Kenya, Kuwait, Lesotho, Malawi, Maldive Islands, Malta, Nigeria, Sierra Leone, Singapore, Somalia (in respect of Somaliland), Southern Yemen, Trinidad and Tobago, Uganda, Tanzania, Zambia.

only five notified succession to the Convention on the High Seas,[8] and four each to the other two Conventions.[9] In addition, two newly independent States, Malawi and Uganda, acceded rather than succeeded to the three Conventions. Hence, only about one third of the possible total number of notifications of succession or accession to those Conventions was received by 31 December 1968.[10]

The record for the Convention on the Continental Shelf is even lower. Since the United Kingdom ratified it on 11 May 1964, eleven territories which this ratification covered had become independent as of December 1967.[11] Of these, only one State (Malta) notified succession and one State (Malawi) accession, a proportion of two to eleven, or only about one sixth of the maximum.[12]

On the other hand, the number of notifications of succession to all four law of the sea Conventions (altogether fourteen) was twice as large as the number of notifications of accession (altogether seven).

The Optional Protocol of Signature concerning the Compulsory Settlement of Disputes, 1958, received one notification of succession (Malta) and three accessions (Malawi, Sierra Leone and Uganda), a total of 20 percent of possible successions or accessions.

C. HUMAN RIGHTS TREATIES

1. *Convention on Genocide, 1948*

This Convention received seventy-three acceptances, of which one was through notification of succession.

The Convention contains an optional colonial clause,[13] pursuant to which Belgium had extended the Convention to the then Belgian Congo and Ruanda-Urundi. Subsequently, only Congo (D.R.) notified succession, while Burundi and Rwanda have notified neither succession nor accession. France ratified the Convention on 14 October 1950 but made no declaration regarding territorial application. Therefore, information about succession has not been elicited from States which were formerly

[8] Jamaica, Malta, Nigeria, Sierra Leone, Trinidad and Tobago.

[9] Jamaica, Nigeria, Sierra Leone, Trinidad and Tobago.

[10] The following States have not so far notified succession or accession to the law of the Sea Conventions:

(a) *The Convention on the Territorial Sea*: Barbados, Botswana, Gambia, Guyana, Kenya, Kuwait, Lesotho, Maldive Islands, Singapore, Somalia (in respect of Somaliland), Southern Yemen, Tanzania, Zambia.

(b) *The Convention on the High Seas*: the above States and Malta.

(c) *The Convention on Fishing*: the above States and Malta.

[11] Barbados, Botswana, Gambia, Guyana, Lesotho, Malawi, Maldive Islands, Malta, Singapore, Southern Yemen, Zambia.

[12] The following States have not notified succession or accession to *The Convention on the Continental Shelf*: Barbados, Botswana, Gambia, Guyana, Lesotho, Maldive Islands, Singapore, Southern Yemen, Zambia.

[13] See art. XII.

French dependent territories. Six of them, however, acceded to the Convention after becoming independent. The United Kingdom has so far not become a party to it. Twenty-five of the former British dependent territories had become independent as of 31 December 1967, but only two of them acceded to it.

2. *Convention on Refugees, 1951*

This Convention received fifty-four acceptances, of which fifteen constituted notifications of succession,[14] twelve from former French territories and three from former British territories.

Pursuant to its optional colonial clause, France extended the Convention on 23 June 1954 to "all territories for the international relations of which France is responsible." Hence, eighteen States formerly under French jurisdiction could have succeeded to the Convention, but only twelve of them notified succession and two of them (Gabon and Madagascar) acceded.[15]

The United Kingdom had extended the Convention to Cyprus, Gambia, Jamaica, Kenya and Somaliland Protectorate on 25 October 1956, to the Federation of Rhodesia and Nyasaland on 11 July 1960, and to Basutoland, Bechuanaland Protectorate and Swaziland on 11 November 1960. Of these, only Cyrpus, Gambia and Jamaica so far have notified succession. Kenya and Tanzania acceded to the Convention. Thus the actual number of notifications of successions and accessions has been less than the possible number of successions.[16]

3. *Convention on the Political Rights of Women, 1953*

This Convention received sixty-one acceptances, of which four constituted notifications of succession.

France ratified the Convention on 22 April 1957. As the Convention contains no colonial clause, its ratification applied in principle to seventeen dependent territories, which later became independent. Of them, four States notified succession,[17] one State signed and ratified it[18] and two acceded to it.[19] Consequently, ten of the former French dependent

---

[14] Algeria, Cameroon, Central African Republic, Congo (B.), Cyprus, Dahomey, Gambia, Guinea, Ivory Coast, Jamaica, Morocco, Niger, Senegal, Togo, Tunisia.

[15] The following four States have so far neither succeeded or acceded: Chad, Mali, Mauritania, Upper Volta.

[16] The following States have so far notified neither succession nor accession: Somalia (in respect of Somaliland), Zambia and Lesotho. (This enumeration does not include States that attained independence after 31 Dec. 1967.)

[17] Central African Republic, Congo (B.), Niger, Senegal.

[18] Gabon. This Convention has no closing date for signature; consequently, it is open for signature and ratification also.

[19] Madagascar, Tunisia.

territories have not notified succession or accession or ratification since becoming independent.

4. *Convention on the Nationality of Married Women, 1957*

It received forty-one acceptances, of which five constituted notifications of succession.

The colonial clause (article 7) obligates States, subject to certain qualifications, to declare the non-metropolitan territories to which the Convention shall apply *ipso facto* as a result of signature, ratification or accession.

Fifteen of the territories to which the United Kingdom extended the Convention in 1958 had become independent as of 31 December 1967. Only five[20] of them notified succession; in addition, two[21] acceded to the Convention. Eight States[22] notified neither succession nor accession to it. New Zealand extended the Convention on 17 December 1958 among others to Western Samoa, which later became independent. Western Samoa has notified neither succession nor accession.

5. *Supplementary Convention on Slavery, 1956*

This Convention received seventy-three acceptances, of which six constituted notifications of succession.[23]

Under the optional colonial clause, the United Kingdom extended this Convention on various dates to fifty dependent territories. Of the eighteen States which had become independent as of 31 December 1967, six States[24] notified succession and three States[25] acceded to the Convention. Nine States[26] have yet to notify succession or accession.

D. Treaties on Narcotic Drugs

The treaties on narcotic drugs in general received a comparatively large number of successions, a factor contributing to their relatively high percentage of acceptance.[27] This can be illustrated by reference to the following two narcotics treaties:

1. *Protocol Bringing Under International Control Drugs Outside the Scope of the Convention of 13 July 1931 for Limiting the*

---

[20] Jamaica, Malaysia, Sierra Leone, Singapore, Trinidad and Tobago.

[21] Uganda, Tanzania.

[22] Barbados, Botswana, Cyprus, Gambia, Guyana, Kenya, Southern Yemen, Zambia.

[23] Cyprus, Jamaica, Malta, Nigeria, Sierra Leone, Trinidad and Tobago.

[24] See note 23.

[25] Kuwait, Tanzania, Uganda.

[26] Barbados, Botswana, Guyana, Gambia, Lesotho, Kenya, Singapore, Somalia (in respect of Somaliland), Zambia.

[27] See in general chap. two.

*Manufacture and Regulating the Distribution of Narcotic Drugs,
as amended by the 1964 Protocol*

This treaty received eighty acceptances, of which eighteen constituted notifications of succession.

Pursuant to its optional colonial clause,[28] Belgium, France, New
Zealand and the United Kingdom extended this treaty to three, twenty-
two, one and forty-one territories, respectively. Forty-two of the sixty-
seven territories had become independent, as of 31 December 1967. Of
the forty-two, only eighteen States notified succession. In addition, Tanzania, Uganda and Upper Volta acceded to the treaty. Accordingly,
twenty-one States have notified neither succession nor accession.[29] Nevertheless, a comparatively large number of States have notifid one or
the other.

2. *Protocol for Limiting and Regulating the Cultivation of the Poppy Plant, 1953*

This treaty received fifty acceptances, of which nine constituted
notifications of succession.[30]

Article 20, the colonial clause, says that "This Protocol shall apply
to all the non-self-governing, trust, colonial and other non-metropolitan
territories . . . except where the previous consent of a non-metropolitan
territory is required by the Constitution of the Party or of the non-
metropolitan territory, or required by custom." France extended the
Protocol on 21 April 1954 to the Territories of the French Union; New
Zealand on 2 November 1956 to Western Samoa; and Belgium on 30
June 1958 to the Belgian Congo and Ruandi-Urundi.

The actual number of notifications of succession or accession to this
Protocol is relatively high, but is less than the possible maximum.[31]

E. TREATIES ON TRANSPORT AND CUSTOMS

1. *Transport*

The Convention on Road Traffic, 1949, received seventy-nine
acceptances, of which fifteen constituted notifications of succession.[32]

---

[28] See art. 8.

[29] Algeria, Barbados, Botswana, Burundi, Chad, Cyprus, Gabon, Gam-
bia, Guinea, Guyana, Kenya, Lesotho, Madagascar, Maldive Islands, Mali,
Malta, Singapore, Southern Yemen, Somalia (in respect of Somaliland),
Western Samoa, Zambia.

[30] Cameroon, Central African Republic, Congo (B.), Congo (D.R.),
Ivory Coast, Madagascar, Niger, Rwanda, Senegal.

[31] For example, Algeria, Burundi, Chad, Dahomey, Gabon, Guinea,
Mali, Mauritania, Togo, Upper Volta, Western Samoa have notified neither
succession nor accession.

[32] Central African Republic, Congo (D.R.), Cyprus, Dahomey, Ivory
Coast, Jamaica, Madagascar, Mali, Malta, Morocco, Niger, Rwanda, Senegal, Sierra Leone, Togo.

Belgium had extended the Convention on 23 April 1954 to the Belgian Congo and the Trust Territory of Ruanda-Urundi. Of the three States, Congo (D.R.), Burundi and Rwanda, Congo (D.R.) and Rwanda notified succession to the treaty. France ratified the Convention on 15 September 1950 and extended it to the French Protectorates of Morocco and Tunisia, all French Overseas Territories, and Togoland and the Cameroons under French Mandate. Of these, twelve States notified succession and three accession to the Convention, while the following six States neither succeeded nor acceded: Cameroon, Chad, Gabon, Guinea, Mauritania and Upper Volta. New Zealand extended the Convention on 29 November 1961 to the Trust Territory of Western Samoa, but the latter, since its independence, has notified neither succession nor accession. The United Kingdom ratified the Convention on 30 August 1950 and subsequently extended it to Aden Colony, British Guiana, Cyprus, Uganda, Jamaica, Trinidad, Gambia, Singapore, Zanzibar, the Federation of Rhodesia and Nyasaland, and Barbados. Of these, four notified succession, and two acceded to it.

Accordingly, although the number of successions or accessions to this treaty is comparatively high, the aggregate is less than the possible number of successions or accessions.

2. *Customs*

The Convention on Commercial Samples, 1952, received forty-nine acceptances, of which eleven constituted notifications of succession.[33] The colonial clause is of the optional form.[34]

Belgium extended the Convention to the Belgian Congo and Ruanda-Urundi. Of the three States, Congo (D.R.) and Rwanda notified succession. Burundi has notified neither succession nor accession; the same is true of Western Samoa, to which the Convention was extended by New Zealand. The United Kingdom has extended it to thirty-two territories, of which seventeen had become independent as of 31 December 1967. Of the latter, nine notified succession and three acceded to it; consequently, five States have notified neither succession nor accession. In all, seven states have failed to notify succession or accession.[35]

The position regarding other treaties on customs is almost similar. For example, the Convention Concerning Customs Facilities, 1954, received sixty-one acceptances, of which nine constituted notifications of succession.[36]

[33] Congo (D.R.), Cyprus, Ghana, Jamaica, Malaysia, Malta, Nigeria, Rwanda, Sierra Leone, Singapore, Trinidad and Tobago.

[34] See art. XIII.

[35] Barbados, Burundi, Gambia, Guyana, Somalia (in respect of Somaliland), Southern Yemen, Western Samoa.

[36] Cyprus, Jamaica, Malaysia, Malta, Nigeria, Rwanda, Sierra Leone, Singapore, Trinidad and Tobago.

Belgium extended the Convention to the Belgian Congo and the Trust Territory of Ruanda-Urundi. Of these, only Rwanda notified succession. The United Kingdom extended the Convention on two different occasions to thirty territories, of which fifteen had become independent as of 31 December 1967. Of the latter, eight notified succession and two acceded; consequently, five States have yet to notify succession or accession.[37] Seven States in all have notified neither succession nor accession.

F. TREATIES ON EDUCATIONAL MATTERS AND OBSCENE PUBLICATIONS

1. *Agreement on the Importation of Educational Matters, 1950*

This treaty received fifty-seven acceptances, of which nine constituted notifications of succession.[38]

The colonial clause in the agreement is of the optional form.[39]

Belgium extended the agreement to the Belgian Congo and the Trust Territory of Ruanda-Urundi, but only Congo (D.R.) and Rwanda notified succession; France extended it to Tunisia, but the latter has not so far notified succession or accession. The United Kingdom has extended it on various occasions to a large number of dependent territories; twenty of these territories had become independent as of 31 December 1967, but only seven States[40] notified succession and four more acceded.[41] Accordingly, nine States to which the United Kingdom had extended the agreement have so far notified neither succession nor accession.[42] In all, eleven States have notified neither succession nor accession.

2. *Convention on Obscene Publications, 1923, as amended by the 1947 Protocol*

This treaty received forty-seven acceptances, of which nine constituted notifications of succession.[43]

The treaty contains no colonial clause.

Belgium has accepted the Convention as of 12 November 1947. Its acceptance would apply to Burundi, Congo (D.R.) and Rwanda, but

---

[37] Barbados, Guyana, Gambia, Kenya, Somalia (in respect of Somaliland).

[38] Congo (D.R.), Cyprus, Ghana, Malaysia, Malta, Nigeria, Rwanda, Sierra Leone, Trinidad and Tobago.

[39] See art. XIII.

[40] Cyprus, Ghana, Malaysia, Malta, Nigeria, Sierra Leone, Trinidad and Tobago.

[41] Cameroon, Kenya, Tanzania, Uganda.

[42] Barbados, Guyana, Gambia, Jamaica, Singapore, Somalia (in respect of Somaliland), Southern Yemen, Togo (in respect of Togoland-U.K. Trust Territory), Zambia.

[43] Congo (D.R.), Cyprus, Ghana, Jamaica, Malaysia, Malta, Nigeria, Sierra Leone, Trinidad and Tobago.

only Congo (D.R.) notified succession. The United Kingdom accepted this treaty on 16 May 1949. Twenty-five States formerly under British jurisdiction would be entitled to succeed to United Kingdom's acceptance; however, only eight States notified succession and three more acceded. Consequently, fourteen States have notified neither succession nor accession,[44] sixteen States in all have failed to notify succession or accession to this treaty.

G. OTHER TREATIES

1. *Convention on the Recovery Abroad of Maintenance, 1956*

This Convention received thirty-two acceptances, none of them through succession.

France ratified this Convention on 24 June 1960 with the declaration that the Convention shall apply to "the territories of the French Republic, namely: the metropolitan departments, the departments of Algeria, the departments of the Oases and of Saoura, the departments of Guadeloupe, Guiana, Martinique and Reunion and the Overseas Territories (St. Pierre and Miquelon, French Somaliland, the Comoro Archipelago, New Caledonia and Dependencies and French Polynesia)." This declaration would entitle only Algeria to succeed to the treaty, which it has not done.

2. *Convention on the Recognition and Enforcement of Foreign Arbitral Awards, 1958*

This Convention received thirty-four acceptances, none of them through succession.

France ratified this treaty on 26 June 1959, declaring at that time that the Convention shall extend to "all the territories of the French Republic." Such declaration would entitle Algeria to succeed, which it has not done.

* * * * *

It appears from the foregoing survey that in general, small States[45] and States that attained independence recently[46] have not yet notified succession. These categories are not mutually exclusive, nor is the delay in or lack of succession confined to such States. Other States which attained independence in the early 1960s have also failed to notify

[44] Barbados, Botswana, Cameroon, Gambia, Guyana, Kenya, Kuwait, Lesotho, Maldive Islands, Somalia (in respect of Somaliland), Southern Yemen, Sudan, Uganda, Zambia. (This enumeration does not include States that attained independence after 31 Dec. 1967.)

[45] For example, Botswana, Gambia, Guyana, Lesotho, Maldive Islands and Western Samoa. (Barbados and Gambia succeeded to one treaty each.)

[46] Southern Yemen and Zambia.

succession either to all treaties[47] or to some treaties[48] previously extended to their territories.

A small number of new States, for example, Algeria,[49] Israel, the East African States (Kenya, Tanzania and Uganda) and Upper Volta, however, chose the mode of accession rather than succession, thus becoming parties to all or some of the old treaties.

III. POSSIBLE CAUSES OF DELAY OR FAILURE FOR NON-SUCCESSION OR NON-ACCESSION

A. AMBIGUITY REGARDING THE LAW OF SUCCESSION

Some States acceded to the old treaties instead of succeeding because they considered the law regarding succession to be somewhat ambiguous and/or not applicable to their situation. The positions taken by Israel, Tanzania, Upper Volta and Madagascar illustrate this point.

1. Israel

Israel considered itself not automatically bound by the multilateral treaties applied in, or extended to, the Territory of Palestine by the Government of the United Kingdom. Its view is based upon, among other grounds, the fact that "there can be no automatic elevation of a dependent territory to the status of a party to a treaty simply because the terms of a treaty may have been made applicable to that territory by the Power in whose hands was entrusted the control of the foreign relations of that dependent territory."[50] However, it acceded to the treaties to which it wanted to become a party, whether or not they were extended to it by the United Kingdom.

2. Tanzania

Tanganyika, before its union with Zanzibar, made a declaration on 9 December 1961 regarding succession to multilateral treaties which stated that "the Government of Tanganyika proposes to review each of them individually and to indicate to the depositary in each case what steps it wishes to take in relation to each such instrument—whether by way of confirmation of termination, confirmation of succession or accession. . ."[51] Although Tanganyika thus left open the mode of acceptance to old treaties, it later in fact chose the method of accession rather than

[47] For example, Burundi, Chad, Kuwait and Mauritania.

[48] For example, Ivory Coast, Mali (succeeded to only one treaty), Togo and Congo (D.R.).

[49] However, Algeria chose the mode of succession to the Convention on Refugees, 1951.

[50] Cited in *Yearbook of the International Law Commission* (1950), vol. II, p. 215; see also United Nations, *Materials on Succession of States* (1967), pp. 38-58.

[51] U.N. Doc. A/CN.4/150, *op. cit.*, note 2, p. 121.

succession. A possible explanation for the choice of accession lies in the "legal uncertainties" the Government of Tanganyika at that time felt about the theory of universal succession.[52] Two other East African States, Kenya and Uganda, have adopted similar positions as regards the multilateral treaties previously extended to their territories.[53]

3. *Upper Volta*

Upper Volta, in replying to the Secretary-General's inquiry about succession, said: "The Upper Volta, as a sovereign independent State, does not acknowledge itself bound by the Agreements signed by France before the Republic of Upper Volta became independent."[54] Like Israel and Tanzania, Upper Volta acceded to some of the old treaties.

4. *Madagascar*

The legal position of Madagascar also seems to reflect the uncertainties it initially felt about succession to treaties previously extended to its territory by France. In replying to the Secretary-General's inquiry about succession, the Foreign Ministry of Madagascar first said:

This, however, is a point of international law on which the highest legal authorities to whom it has been submitted have been unable to give a conclusive opinion. Consequently it seems hard to formulate any principle, and each particular case should be examined with care.[55]

Later, however, the Foreign Ministry stated:

After examining the question, the Malagasy Government considers that it ought in principle to acknowledge itself bound by the Agreements and Conventions entered into in its name by France before the Malagasy Republic became independent. Although this principle has been accepted, it nevertheless seems essential that in the case of each Convention a formal notification should be sent to you by which the Malagasy Government would declare itself bound.[56]

B. Non-Application of Certain Treaties in Dependent Territories

Some of the States based their non-succession on the ground that the treaties concerned were not extended to their territories by the predecessor Government. Ivory Coast and Togo, for instance, declared that they do

[52] See "Treaties and Succession of States and Government in Tanzania" by E. E. Seaton and S. T. M. Maliti in *African Conference on International Law and African Problems* (Lagos, 1967), pp. 76-97.

[53] For minor differences between Tanzania's position and Uganda's, see Seaton and Maliti, *op. cit.*, p. 78.

[54] U.N. Doc. A/CN.4/150, *op. cit.*, note 2, p. 119.

[55] *Ibid.*, p. 117.

[56] *Ibid.*

not consider themselves bound by the Convention on the Political Rights of Women, as it had not been extended to their territories by France.[57]

Congo (D.R.) delayed succession to three customs treaties,[58] stating that they were continuing research as to whether the treaties concerned had ever been published in the legislation of Congo.[59]

IV. MEASURES AND PROCEDURES FACILITATING SUCCESSION

A. ON THE NATIONAL LEVEL

1. *Succession versus accession*

Of the two modes by which new States become parties to an old treaty, succession or accession, the former has certain advantages. Through succession, a State becomes a party from the date of its independence; through accession, only from the date of accession.[60] Consequently, succession maintains continuity in the operation of the treaty, whereas accession involves a break in its operation. Secondly, the procedure for notification of succession is usually less formal and more simple;[61] accession requires more complex and time-consuming procedures. Thirdly, the difficulties which some new States are facing due to lack of expertise and personnel may be alleviated by adopting the relatively simpler method of succession.

2. *Clarification of the issue of territorial application*

Some States have declined to succeed to treaties which contain no colonial clauses on the ground that their predecessor Governments had not specifically extended the treaties to territories. This attitude seems to be based on a misunderstanding. It is by now established practice that acceptance by a State of a treaty containing no colonial clause would in principle apply to all its dependent territories. In fact, the omission of colonial clauses in more recent treaties has been because specific extension of United Nations treaties to dependent territories is not necessary for the treaty to be applicable to them.

[57] U.N. Doc. A/CN.4/150, *op. cit.*, note 2, p. 116 (Ivory Coast), p. 119 (Togo).

    [58] (a) Convention on Customs Facilities for Touring, 1954.
        (b) Additional Protocol on Tourist Publicity Documents, 1954.
        (c) Customs Convention on Private Road Vehicles, 1954.

    [59] U.N. Doc. A/CN.4/150, *op. cit.* note 2, p. 115.

    [60] See, however, Tanzania's declaration of 9 Dec. 1961, which stated: "During such interim period of review any party to a multilateral treaty which has prior to independence been applied or extended to Tanganyika may, on a basis of reciprocity, rely as against Tanganyika on the terms of such treaty." See *United Nations Materials on Succession of States* (New York, 1967), p. 178.

    [61] States may notify succession by a letter from either the Head of the State, the Government or the Minister of Foreign Affairs.

3. *The question of a devolution agreement relating to United Nations treaties*

Experience indicates that devolution agreements have facilitated succession to United Nations treaties. Ceylon, Ghana, Nigeria, Sierra Leone, Jamaica, Trinidad and Tobago, Malta and Malaysia, among others, concluded such agreements with the United Kingdom and subsequently notified "definitive" succession to most of the treaties that were previously extended to their territories. This largely contributed to the relatively high records of acceptance of these States.[62] The question for consideration is whether countries which are in the process of attaining independence should enter into devolution agreements in respect of United Nations treaties. One State which in the past declined to enter into such an agreement argued that "an inheritance agreement would probably not be able by itself to enable [a State] to insist that third States discharge towards [it] the obligations which they assumed under the ·original treaty."[63] In another context it was argued that a new State would usually not have the opportunity to study the respective treaties before entering into such an agreement.[64] These two objections do not seem to apply to multilateral treaties, although they may be valid in the case of some bilateral treaties. Third States do not seem to have questioned the devolution of multilateral treaties; furthermore succession to United Nations treaties may, in view of the importance of their subject matters and methods of their adoption, be considered differently from bilateral treaties.

B. UNITED NATIONS PROCEDURES AND ASSISTANCE

As mentioned before, under the present United Nations procedures a new State is not considered a party to a treaty until it notifies the Secretary-General of "definitive" succession, regardless of whether a devolution agreement exists. This procedure could conceivably be modified if such an agreement does exist, as the States concerned have already expressed their consent to succession.

A legal opinion given by the Secretariat on the issue of succession by Jamaica to rights and obligations arising from the territorial application of

---

[62] Nineteen of the 27 acceptances by Trinidad and Tobago are due to succession; so are 19 of 26 acceptances by Sierra Leone; 18 of the 26 acceptances by Jamaica; 16 of the 23 acceptances by Nigeria; 10 of the 27 acceptances by Ghana; 12 of the 16 acceptances by Cyprus; 10 of the 22 acceptances by Malaysia and 15 of the 20 acceptances by Malta.

[63] See the policy statement made in the National Assembly of Tanganyika by the then Prime Minister, Julius Nyerere. Quoted in Seaton and Maliti, *op. cit.*, p. 77.

[64] This point was made by Mr. Seaton in the *African Conference on International Law and African Problems, op. cit.*, p. 21.

the Convention on Refugees, 1951, may be referred to here. On 7 August 1962 Jamaica entered into a devolution agreement with the United Kingdom, whereby it assumed the rights and obligations for treaties previously extended to its territory. The question arose whether Jamaica had become a party to the Convention on Refugees. The Secretariat's legal opinion was:

> We have reached the conclusion that the High Commissioner may consider that Jamaica has become a party to the 1951 Convention by assuming the obligations and responsibilities of the United Kingdom under that Convention in so far as it may be held to have application to Jamaica.[65]

When there is no devolution agreement, other procedures may be considered. It has been the general practice of the International Labour Organisation to secure acceptance by the new States of the I.L.O. Conventions applied in their territories at the time of admission to membership in the Organisation.[66] Although such a procedure obviously cannot be applied in the United Nations, the latter may consider taking action subsequent to the admission of the new Members, with a view to securing successions. Moreover, the United Nations may take up periodically the problem of succession to United Nations treaties by the new States and recommend measures for expediting succession.

New States might be provided with such background information about the treaties to assist them in appreciating the objectives, scope and purposes of United Nations treaties. Studies prepared by the Secretariat on *The Work of the International Law Commission,* on human rights instruments and on other conventions could be supplied to the States at the time of eliciting information about succession. At present, the new States are supplied only with the lists and texts of treaties; background studies, however, would provide them the data necessary for reaching more prompt decisions on the succession issue.

As mentioned in chapter three, requests have been made by some new States for the services of legal advisors and experts to assist on the question of succession to treaties, among other things. This too may have the effect of increasing adherence through succession.

---

[65] *United Nations Juridical Year Book* (1963), p. 181.

[66] C. W. Jenks, "State succession in respect of law-making treaties," The *British Year Book of International Law,* vol. 29 (1952), pp. 105-144; see also J. F. McMahon, "The legislative techniques of the International Labour Organisation," The *British Year Book of International Law,* vol. 41 (1965-66), pp. 1-102, especially pp. 73-77.

CHAPTER EIGHT

RELATION OF RESERVATIONS TO ACCEPTANCE

I. INTRODUCTION

It is reasonable to assume that the right to make reservations to multilateral treaties facilitates their wider acceptance. As observed by the International Law Commission in its commentary on draft articles on the Law of Treaties:

> . . . a power to formulate reservations must in the nature of things tend to make it easier for some States to execute the act necessary to bind themselves finally to participating in the treaty and therefore tend to promote a greater measure of universality in the application of the treaty. . .[1]

The Commission further observed that "when today the number of the negotiating States may be upwards of one hundred States with very diverse cultural, economic and political conditions, it seems necessary to assume that the power to make reservations without the risk of being totally excluded by the objection of one or even of a few States may be a factor in promoting a more general acceptance of multilateral treaties."[2] Finally, the Commission was of the view that the rule calculated to promote the widest possible acceptance of treaties may be most suitable to the needs of the international community.[3]

However, it has been said on at least one occasion that the assumption that reservations facilitate ratifications and accessions lacks statistical confirmation. The United Kingdom stated in the *Genocide* case that "a statistical investigation might well reveal that the average number of ratifications or accessions to Pan-American Union Conventions, pro-

---

[1] See *Official Records of the General Assembly, 21st session, Supplement No. 9* (A/6309/Rev.1), p. 38.

[2] *Ibid.*

[3] *Ibid.*

portionately to the number of possible participants, is no greater than, or is even less than in the case of other conventions to which the Pan-American system is not applied."[4] Although this chapter will not provide the kind of statistical comparison suggested by the United Kingdom, it will show that of the treaties surveyed, those which permit reservations, or do not prohibit reservations, have received proportionately larger acceptances than treaties which either do not permit reservations to a part or whole of the treaty, or which contain only one substantial clause, making reservations unlikely. It must, however, be borne in mind that some of the treaties which received a relatively large number of acceptances might have been widely accepted, even if there were restrictions on the power to make reservations or declarations that amount to reservations.

Apart from the general question of whether reservations promote acceptances, there is the important question of the extent to which reservations made to multilateral treaties have actually reduced the legal effect of provisions of the treaty in their application. The International Law Commission, in its 1951 report, had the following to say: "It is also desirable to maintain uniformity in the obligations of all the parties to a multilateral convention, and it may often be more important to maintain the integrity of a convention than to aim, at any price, at the widest possible acceptance of it."[5]

The survey which follows will throw some light on the actual effects of reservations by examining the nature and extent of reservations made to a representative sample of treaties.

II. SURVEY OF THE NATURE AND EXTENT OF RESERVATIONS

The treaties surveyed here fall into three categories: 1) those which permit reservations without any special limit; 2) those which do not permit reservations to certain clauses; and 3) those which do not permit any substantive reservations. There is another category of treaties, those which contain in effect only one substantive clause and to which any reservations would ordinarily defeat the very purpose and operation of the treaty.

According to the article 2(d) of the Vienna Convention on the Law of Treaties, 1969, a "reservation means a unilateral statement, however phrased or named, made by a State, when signing, ratifying, accepting or approving or acceding to a treaty, whereby it purports to exclude or to vary the legal effect of certain provisions of the treaty in their application

---

[4] International Court of Justice, *Reservations to the Convention on the Prevention and Punishment of the Crime of Genocide,* Advisory Opinion of 28 May 1951, Pleadings, Oral Arguments, Documents, p. 60.

[5] *The Yearbook of the International Law Commission* (1951), vol. II, p. 129.

to that State."[6] This definition of reservations has been used as a guideline in enumerating reservations in this survey.

A. TREATIES WHICH PERMIT RESERVATIONS WITHOUT ANY SPECIAL LIMIT

1. *Convention on the Territorial Sea, 1958*

The treaty has been accepted by thirty-six States, with reservations by fourteen[7] States upon either signature or ratification. These reservations are of different kinds and with varying limiting effects on the treaty. One State has made a reservation in respect of article 24 concerning the contiguous zone. Another made a reservation in respect of article 12 (demarcation of coastlines by States opposite or adjacent to each other) and also paragraphs 2 and 3 of article 24. Eight States have, in respect of article 20, stated that Government ships in foreign territorial waters have immunity and that the measures mentioned in the articles can be applied by the coastal State only with the consent of the flag State. These States have also tried to interpret article 23 to the effect that it does not establish the right of innocent passage for warships through the territorial waters, nor the right of a coastal State to establish procedures for the authorization of the passage of foreign warships through its territorial waters. Ten States have made objections to the reservations made by other States, thus limiting treaty relations with those States.

2. *Convention on the High Seas, 1958*

Forty-three States have accepted the treaty, while thirteen States[8] have made reservations. Ten States have made reservations to article 9 to the effect that the principle of international law according to which a ship on the high seas is not subject to any jurisdiction except that of the flag State applies without restriction to all Government ships.

Another State's reservations concern the meaning of the terms "territorial sea" and "internal waters." Ten States have objected to the reservations made by a number of States.

---

[6] See also art. 19 (Formulation of Reservations), art. 20 (Acceptance of and Objection to Reservations), art. 21 (Legal Effects of Reservations and of Objections to Reservations).

[7] Bulgaria, Byelorussian SSR, Colombia, Czechoslovakia, Hungary, Iran, Italy, Mexico, Romania, Tunisia, Ukrainian SSR, USSR, United Kingdom and Venezuela. (Colombia, Iran and Tunisia have not yet ratified the treaty.)

[8] Albania, Bulgaria, Byelorussian SSR, Czechoslovakia, Hungary, Indonesia, Iran, Mexico, Poland, Romania, Ukrainian SSR, USSR and the United Kingdom. (Iran is not yet a party.)

3. *Vienna Convention on Diplomatic Relations, 1961*

Eighty-two States have accepted the treaty, and eighteen States[9] have made reservations and declarations. Two States objected to articles 48 and 50 concerning participation in the treaty. Four States made similar declarations and in addition made reservations to article 11, paragraph 1, to the effect that any difference of opinion with regard to the size of a diplomatic mission should be settled between the sending State and the reserving State. Reservations by many States relate to the privileges and immunities of administrative and technical staff of the mission and of private servants, as well as to questions of travelling tax and appointment of nationals of such States to diplomatic staff. Ten States made objections to some of the reservations or declarations.

4. *Vienna Convention on Consular Relations*, 1963

Accepted by thirty-three States, this Convention is subject to reservations by four States.[10] Two States objected to the limitations on participation contained in articles 74 and 76. Another State, through its reservation, refused to accept that part of article 31, paragraph 4, which refers to expropriation of consular premises, since the clause is in contradiction to its political constitution. One State indicated that it would have no treaty relation with another State party which it did not recognize. The same State also made reservations to articles 46, 49, 62 and 65, thereby reducing its obligations under the treaty. The United Kingdom, which has not yet accepted the treaty, made reservations at the time of signature concerning articles 43 and 44. Two other States have objected to the reservations made by others.

5. *Convention on the Prevention and Punishment of the Crime of Genocide, 1948*

Seventy-three States have accepted the Convention and nineteen States[11] have made reservations. Some of these reservations have been objected to by eleven States.[12] Almost all the reservations indicate that the reserving State is not bound by article 9, which confers on the International Court of Justice jurisdiction in all disputes relating to the Convention. Other reservations relate either to article 6, conferring

---

[9] Bulgaria, Byelorussian SSR, Cambodia, Cuba, Greece, Hungary, Iraq, Japan, Malta, Mongolia, Morocco, Nepal, Portugal, Romania, Ukrainian SSR, USSR, United Arab Republic and Venezuela.

[10] Cuba, Czechoslovakia, Mexico and United Arab Republic.

[11] Albania, Algeria, Argentina, Bulgaria, Burma, Byelorussian SSR, Czechoslovakia, Finland, Hungary, India, Mongolia, Morocco, Philippines, Poland, Romania, Spain, Ukrainian SSR, USSR and Venezuela.

[12] Australia, Belgium, Brazil, Ceylon, China, Cuba, Ecuador, Greece, Netherlands, Norway and Republic of Vietnam.

jurisdiction on the proposed international penal tribunal, or to substantive provisions of the Convention.

6. *Convention on the Political Rights of Women, 1953*

Of the sixty-one States parties to the treaty, twenty-nine[13] have made reservations or declarations. Twelve States have objected to one or more of these reservations. Fifteen States have made reservations to article 9, thus refusing to accept the jurisdiction of the International Court of Justice except when agreed to by all the parties to the dispute. Reservations by nine States restrict the operation of article 3 insofar as recruitment to armed or public services is concerned. Other reservations stated that some of the provisions of the treaty can be implemented subject to the supremacy of national constitutions or other applicable laws.

7. *Convention relating to the Status of Refugees, 1951*

Fifty-four States have accepted the treaty and twenty-eight States[14] have made reservations. This is exclusive of the option exercised by fifty-three States in regard to the interpretation of the term "events occurring before 1 January 1951." Some of the original reservations were later withdrawn by six States, who still maintained other reservations. By their reservations, thirteen States excluded or modified the application of article 17 concerning wage-earning employment. A number of States reserved their position in regard to the application of article 24, which requires contracting parties to accord to refugees the same treatment as is accorded to nationals in respect of social security and labour legislation. Other articles to which reservations have been made by one or more States include 1, 7, 8, 9, 11, 12, 14, 15, 23, 25, 26, 28, 31, 32, 34, 42. In fact, there are very few articles of the Convention to which reservations have not been made by more than one State.

8. *Single Convention on Narcotic Drugs, 1961*

This treaty has been accepted by sixty-six States, of which fifteen States[15] made reservations or declarations.

[13] Albania, Argentina, Belgium, Bulgaria, Byelorussian SSR, Canada, Czechoslovakia, Denmark, Ecuador, Finland, Guatemala, Hungary, India, Indonesia, Ireland, Italy, Malta, Mexico, Mongolia, Nepal, New Zealand, Pakistan, Poland, Romania, Sierra Leone, Tunisia, Ukrainian SSR, USSR and the United Kingdom. (Mexico has not yet ratified the treaty.)

[14] Australia, Austria, Belgium, Brazil, Cyprus, Denmark, Ecuador, Finland, France, Gambia, Greece, Holy See, Ireland, Israel, Italy, Jamaica, Liechtenstein, Luxembourg, Madagascar, Monaco, Netherlands, New Zealand, Norway, Portugal, Sweden, Switzerland, Turkey and the United Kingdom.

[15] Algeria, Argentina, Bulgaria, Burma, Byelorussian SSR, Czechoslovakia, Hungary, India, Indonesia, Netherlands, Pakistan, Poland, Ukrainian SSR, USSR and United Arab Republic. (Indonesia has not yet ratified the treaty.)

Five States either did not accept the jurisdiction of the International Court of Justice or modified the applicability of its jurisdiction. Other reservations were meant to safeguard certain transitional interests of the States or to declare that the Convention shall not purport to exercise control over the actions of States which are not parties to the treaty. Some other reservations were policy declarations regarding non-recognition of certain States, thus implying that the treaty should not operate between the reserving State and the unrecognized State or Government.

9. *Convention on Road Traffic, 1949*

Seventy-nine States have accepted the treaty and thirty-seven States[16] have made reservations and declarations. Most of these reservations state that in accordance with article 2, paragraph 1, annexes 1 and 2 are excluded from the application of the Convention. Other reservations were minor in character, though they modified the application of some articles.

10. *Convention concerning Customs Facilities for Touring, 1954*

Of Sixty-one States accepting the treaty, sixteen[17] have made reservations. These reservations seek to reinterpret various provisions of the treaty concerning definition of a tourist, applicability of arbitration procedures, rights to make special rules outside the Convention, etc.

11. *Convention on the Recognition and Enforcement of Foreign Arbitral Awards, 1958*

This Convention, accepted by thirty-four States, has been subject to reservations by twenty-five States.[18] The majority of the reservations are to the effect that States will apply the Convention in accordance with the first sentence of article 1(3) only to the recognition and enforcement of arbitral awards made in the territory of another contracting State. But six States have made declarations providing for application of the Conven-

---

[16] Australia, Botswana, Bulgaria, Chile, Cyprus, Czechoslovakia, Denmark, Dominican Republic, Finland, France, Ghana, Guatemala, Hungary, India, Ireland, Israel, Jamaica, Japan, Malawi, Malaysia, Malta, Monaco, Netherlands, New Zealand, Norway, Philippines, Portugal, Romania, San Marino, Senegal, Sierra Leone, South Africa, Sweden, Trinidad and Tobago, USSR, United Kingdom and Venezuela.

[17] Algeria, Bulgaria, Cuba, Denmark, Finland, Ghana, Haiti, Hungary, Poland, Romania, Sweden, Syria, Tanzania, Uganda, USSR, and United Arab Republic.

[18] Argentina, Austria, Bulgaria, Byelorussian SSR, Central African Republic, Czechoslovakia, Ecuador, Federal Republic of Germany, France, Hungary, India, Japan, Madagascar, Morocco, Netherlands, Norway, Philippines, Poland, Romania, Switzerland, Tanzania, Trinidad and Tobago, Tunisia, Ukrainian SSR, and USSR. (Argentina has not ratified the Convention.)

tion in respect of non-contracting States to the extent to which these States grant reciprocal treatment.

B. TREATIES WHICH DO NOT PERMIT RESERVATIONS TO CERTAIN CLAUSES

1. *Convention on Fishing and Conservation of the Living Resources of the High Seas, 1958*

This treaty does not permit reservations to articles 6, 7, 9, 10, 11 and 12. These articles deal with the special rights of coastal States to the high seas adjacent to their territorial sea (6 and 7) and provide the machinery for the settlement of disputes which may arise under articles 4, 5, 6, 7 and 8 of the Convention. Twenty-seven States have accepted the treaty. Two reservations have been made to the treaty. First, Denmark does not consider itself bound by the last sentence in article 2, which states that "Conservation programmes should be formulated with a view to securing in the first place a supply of food for human consumption." The second reservation is by the United States of America and relates to the principle of "abstention."

2. *Convention on the Continental Shelf, 1958*

Reservations are not permitted to articles 1, 2 and 3, which define the term "continental shelf" and enumerate the coastal States' rights and limitations thereof. The treaty has been accepted by thirty-nine States, with reservations and declarations by three accepting States: France, Venezuela and Yugoslavia, and statements of understanding by Federal Republic of Germany and Iran, which have not yet ratified the treaty. The declarations by France relate to articles 1, 2, 4, 5 and 6, even though reservations are not permitted to articles 1 and 2. Reservations by Venezuela and Yugoslavia apply to article 6. Objections to the reservations by Venezuela and Yugoslavia apply to article 6. Objections to the reservations made by Iran have been made by France, the Netherlands and the United States of America. Similarly, the French declarations have been objected to by the Netherlands, Thailand, the United Kingdom, the United States of America and Yugoslavia.

3. *International Convention on the Elimination of All Forms of Racial Discrimination, 1965*

While not excluding reservations to a specified article, the Convention in article 20 (2) states that "a reservation incompatible with the object and purpose of this Convention shall not be permitted, nor shall a reservation the effect of which would inhibit the operation of any of the bodies established by this Convention be allowed. A reservation shall be considered incompatible if at least two-thirds of the States Parties to this Convention object to it." Twenty-seven States have accepted the treaty and nine of these have made reservations. Eleven signatory States which have not yet ratified the treaty have also made reservations and declarations. A number of these reservations relate to the jurisdiction of the International Court of Justice.

There are many other conventions like those relating to the Status of Refugees, Status of Stateless Persons and the Reduction of Statelessness which do not permit reservations to most of the substantive clauses.

C. Treaties Which do not Permit Any Substantive Reservations

Protocol for Limiting and Regulating the Cultivation of the Poppy Plant, etc., 1953

Except for certain transitional measures listed in article 19, no other reservations are permitted to this Protocol. Fifty States have accepted the treaty, with declarations by five States regarding article 19.

In most of the conventions concluded under the auspices of the Economic Commission for Europe, except for the clause relating to settlement of disputes, no other reservations are permitted. Similarly, the Convention regarding the Measurement and Registration of Vessels employed in Inland Navigation for States within the geographical scope of the Economic Commission for Asia and the Far East does not permit any reservations. The International Convention on Broadcasting Organizations, 1961, does not permit any reservations. Ten States have so far ratified this treaty. Some of the ratifying States have made declarations about the applicability of certain provisions.

D. Other Treaties

There are other treaties, considered in this survey, which contain in effect only one substantive clause or idea. These include the Optional Protocol of signature concerning the Compulsory Settlement of Disputes (relating to the law of the sea Conventions), the two Optional Protocols concerning Acquisition of Nationality (relating to the Conventions on Diplomatic and Consular Relations) and the two Optional Protocols concerning the Compulsory Settlement of Disputes (relating to the Diplomatic and Consular Conventions). These treaties are not easily susceptible to reservations, since any such substantial reservations would nullify the effect of the treaty. An anlysis of the official records of the diplomatic conferences which drew up these conventions and optional protocols seems to indicate that if the substance of the protocols had been made a part of the main convention, a number of States would have found it necessary to make reservations in accepting these treaties.

III. EFFECTS OF RESERVATIONS

The foregoing survey suggests that while a variety of reservations have been made to substantive clauses of treaties, affecting their application, many of them appear to have limited or marginal significance. One may infer that in some of these cases, the States would have accepted without reservations if reservations were not permitted, but this of course cannot be factually demonstrated.

A. EFFECTS OF RESERVATIONS REGARDING SUBSTANTIVE CLAUSES

It has been shown that in a number of treaties which permit reservations, the reservations relate to the applicability and operation of the substantive provisions of the treaty. Such reservations obviously limit the application of the treaty, and in cases where other States parties have objected to the reservations, the treaty as a whole, or the parts objected to, is not operative between the reserving and objecting States. In this respect, the reservation can be viewed as impairing the general applicability of the treaty. For example, in the group of "codification" treaties relating to the law of the sea, about one third of the States had made reservations in respect of one or more major provision.

The extent and implications of reservations made to other treaties vary as far as substantive clauses of the treaties are concerned.[19] It has not been possible to find a pattern of State behaviour in the nature and frequency of reservations to substantive clauses. There is no discernible common ground. One is left only with the obvious conclusion that the motives and objectives of making reservations to substantive provisions of treaties depend on the particular subject matter of the treaty, and that they bear a relation to the attitude of States and to national law and policy pertaining to the specific provisions of the treaty.

B. EFFECTS OF RESERVATIONS AND DECLARATIONS CONCERNING NON-RECOGNITION

Two different types of reservations are made by States to make clear their position regarding recognition of a particular State or States which are or may be States parties to a treaty. The first type of reservation is to the effect that acceptance of a treaty in no way implies the recognition of another State which is also eligible to be a State party, and that no treaty relations will arise between the reserving State and the State which is not recognized by it. The second type of reservation relates to policy statements by States parties in regard to the application of treaties by administering powers to the territories under their administration.

C. EFFECTS OF RESERVATIONS RELATING TO "DISPUTES-SETTLEMENT" CLAUSES

A relatively large number of reservations have been made by States in respect of the "Final Clauses" which provide for the settlement of disputes arising from the interpretation or application of treaties. These States exhibit a definite pattern of behaviour in regard to the acceptance of the compulsory jurisdiction of the International Court of Justice or

---

[19] See Section II above.

other arbitral bodies in dealing with disputes arising from the operation of a treaty. It has often been stated that if these reservations regarding the compulsory jurisdiction of the International Court of Justice had not been permitted, the States might have found it difficult to become parties to the treaty concerned. The fact that many States have made reservations to the jurisdiction clause in a number of treaties, and also the fact that they have not accepted treaties like the Optional Protocols drawn up specifically for the function of settlement of disputes, is relevant to this conclusion.

ANNEX I : QUESTIONNAIRE

(Note: All questions do not apply equally to all countries. The questions are to be a basis for personal interview or discussion).

A. GENERAL

1. Is it necessary for your Government to obtain prior legislative approval or consent before it ratifies or accedes to a multilateral treaty?
2. Should you consider it necessary to obtain prior legislative approval, what measures have you taken in respect of the United Nations treaties? How many treaties are pending before the legislative organ?
3. How often is legislative approval sought? Regularly or on *ad hoc* basis?
4. Is there any section or person in the Ministry or Department of External Affairs whose function it is to study and recommend action leading to acceptance of multilateral treaties?
5. When the subject matter of a treaty is of interest or concern to more than one department, is there any co-ordinating procedure to resolve inter-departmental differences?
6. What procedures, if any, exist in your country to co-ordinate differences among legislative committees concerned with the approval of multilateral treaties?
7. Where does the resistance lie in regard to acceptance? Specify, if possible, the objections in the context of the several groups of treaties.
8. What is the role played by interested parties outside the Government in either promoting or hindering acceptance?
9. a. What is the publicity given to multilateral treaties in your country?
   b. Are they translated into your official language?

B. FORMAL CLAUSES

1. What obstacles have you met in ratifying those multilateral treaties which you had already signed?

157

2. Would a simplified procedure of acceptance speed up and/or promote acceptance?
   a. Do you consider that the present method of acceptance (signature and ratification, or accession) delays acceptance?
   b. What methods would you suggest for simplifying acceptance of treaties?
3. a. What are the effects of the compromissary or "disputes" clause in a particular multilateral treaty on your acceptance?
   b. Would it make any difference if the "disputes" clause were contained in a separate protocol?
   c. What special problems, if any, exist in regard to accepting multilateral treaties dealing with settlement of disputes, such as the optional Protocols concerning the Compulsory Settlement of Disputes?
4. a. What are the effects of reservation clauses on acceptance? Does a liberal doctrine in regard to reservations affect your acceptance one way or the other?
   b. What are the effects of reservation of other States parties to a multilateral treaty on your acceptance?

C. FEDERAL-STATE RELATIONS

1. To what extent have federal-state relations in your country operated as an impediment to all or certain classes of treaties? Specify the treaties in which the problem has been acute.
2. What machinery exists in your country to co-ordinate the different points of views of federal and state governments?
3. Has the device of "federal" clause in multilateral treaties alleviated difficulties arising from the federal problem?

D. RELATIONS BETWEEN REGIONAL AND UNITED NATIONS TREATIES

To what extent do regional multilateral treaties affect acceptance of United Nations treaties?

E. ADMINISTRATIVE PROBLEMS

Is there an adequate number of administrative and legal personnel in your government to deal with problems relating to acceptance of multilateral treaties? If there is not, what kind of technical assistance would help to promote ratification?

F. POLITICO-ECONOMIC PROBLEMS

1. a. Are there any political difficulties (internal or inter-regional) affecting acceptance of multilateral treaties?
   b. To what extent do political changes in government affect the acceptance of treaties?
2. To what extent do domestic, social, economic, cultural and religious factors affect acceptance of multilateral treaties generally and in particular in certain types of treaties?

ANNEX II

STATUS OF CERTAIN MULTILATERAL TREATIES AS OF 31 DECEMBER 1968

No.	Name of Treaty	Vote on Adoption	No. of Signatures without Ratification	No. of Parties at Present	Entry into Force
1	Convention on the Territorial Sea, 29 April 1958	61 to none, with 2 abstentions	23	36	10 Sept. 1964
2	Convention on the High Seas, 29 April 1958	65 to none, with 1 abstention	23	43	30 Sept. 1962
3	Convention on Fishing, 29 April 1958	45 to 1, with 18 abstentions	23	27	20 Mar. 1966
4	Convention on the Continental Shelf, 29 April 1958	57 to 3, with 8 abstentions	24	39	10 June 1964
5	Optional Protocol of Signature concerning the Compulsory Settlement of Disputes, 29 April 1958	52 to none, with 13 abstentions	17	21	30 Sept. 1962
6	Convention on Diplomatic Relations, 18 April 1961	72 to none, with 1 abstention	17	82	24 Apr. 1964
7	Optional Protocol concerning the Compulsory Settlement of Disputes, 18 April 1961	63 to 3, with 9 abstentions	13	33	24 Apr. 1964

No.	Name of Treaty	Vote on Adoption	No. of Signatures without Ratification	No. of Parties at Present	Entry into Force
8	Convention on Consular Relations, 24 April 1963	Unanimously	36	33	19 Mar. 1967
9	Optional Protocol concerning the Compulsory Settlement of Disputes, 24 April 1963	—	31	11	19 Mar. 1967
10	Convention on Genocide, 9 December 1948	Unanimously	5	73	12 Jan. 1951
11	Convention on the Political Rights of Women, 20 December 1952	46 to none, with 11 abstentions	10	61	7 July 1954
12	Supplementary Convention on Slavery, etc., 30 April 1956	40 to none, with 3 abstentions	6	73	30 Apr. 1957
13	Convention on Racial Discrimination, 21 December 1965	106 to none, with 1 abstention	48	27	4 Jan. 1969
14	Agreement on the Importation of Educational Matters, 17 June 1950	Unanimously	8	57	21 May 1952
15	Convention on Transit Trade of Land-Locked States, 8 July 1965	46 to none, with 7 abstentions	20	17	9 June 1967
16	Convention on Foreign Arbitral Awards, 10 June 1958	35 to none, with 4 abstentions	9	34	7 June 1959

ANNEX III
CHART OF SIGNATURE OR ACCEPTANCE OF GENERAL MULTILATERAL TREATIES
(AS OF 31 DECEMBER 1968)

UNTS, Vol. 98, p. 101 (*Convention on White Slave Traffic, 1910, as amended by the 1949 Protocol*).

XXV. Convention for the Suppression of the Traffic in Persons and of the Exploitation of the Prostitution of Others, 1950, *UNTS*, Vol. 96, p. 271 (*Convention on the Traffic in Persons, 1950*).

XXVI. Convention on the Political Rights of Women, 1952, *UNTS*, Vol. 193, p. 135 (*Convention on the Political Rights of Women, 1952*).

XXVII. Convention on the Nationality of Married Women, 1957, *UNTS*, Vol. 309, p. 65 (*Convention on the Nationality of Married Women, 1957*).

XXVIII. Convention on Consent to Marriage, Minimum Age for Marriage and Registration of Marriage, 1962, *UNTS*, Vol. 521, p. 231 (*Convention on Consent to Marriage, 1962*).

XXIX. Slavery Convention, 1926, and amended by the Protocol, 1953, *UNTS*, Vol. 212, p. 17 (*Convention on Slavery, 1926, as amended by the 1953 Protocol*).

XXX. Supplementary Convention on the Abolition of Slavery, the Slave Trade, and Institutions and Practices similar to Slavery, 1956, *UNTS*, Vol. 266, p. 3 (*Supplementary Convention on Slavery, 1956*).

XXXI. Convention on the International Right of Correction, 1953, *UNTS*, Vol. 435, p. 191 (*Convention on the Right of Correction, 1953*).

XXXII. Convention for the Suppression of the Circulation of, and Traffic in, Obscene Publications, 1923, and amended by the Protocol, 1947, *UNTS*, Vol. 46, p. 201 (*Convention on Obscene Publications, 1923, as amended by the 1947 Protocol*).

XXXIII. Agreement for the Suppression of the Circulation of Obscene Publications, 1910, and amended by the Protocol, 1949, *UNTS*, Vol. 47, p. 159, (*Agreement on Obscene Publications, 1910, as amended by the 1949 Protocol*).

XXXIV. Agreement for Facilitating the International Circulation of Visual and Auditory Materials of an Educational, Scientific and Cultural Character with Protocol, 1949, *UNTS*, Vol. 197, p. 3 (*Agreement on Circulation of Visual and Auditory Materials, 1949*).

XXXV. Agreement on the importation of Educational, Scientific and Cultural Materials with Annexed Protocol, 1950, *UNTS*, Vol. 131, p. 25 (*Agreement on the Importation of Educational Materials, 1950*).

XXXVI. International Convention for the Protection of Performers, Producers of Phonograms and Broadcasting Organisations, 1961, *UNTS*, Vol. 496, p. 43 (*Convention for the Protection of Performers, 1961*).

XXXVII. International Opium Convention, 1925, and amended by the Protocol, 1946, E/NT/2, (*Opium Convention, 1925, as amended by the 1946 Protocol*).

XXXVIII. Convention for Limiting the Manufacture and Regulating the Distribution of Narcotic Drugs, 1931, and amended by the Protocol, 1946, E/NT/3, (*Convention on Narcotic Drugs, 1931, as amended by the 1946 Protocol*).

XXXIX. Convention for the Suppression of the Illicit Traffic in Dangerous Drugs, 1936, and amended by the Protocol, 1946 (*Convention on Dangerous Drugs, 1936, as amended by the 1946 Protocol*).

XL. Protocol Bringing under International Control Drugs outside the Scope of the Convention of 1931 for Limiting the Manufacture and Regulating the Distribution of Narcotic Drugs, and amended by the Protocol, 1948, *UNTS*, Vol. 44, p. 227 (*Protocol on Narcotic Drugs, as amended by the 1948 Protocol*).

XLI. Protocol for Limiting and Regulating the Cultivation of the Poppy Plant, the Production of, International and Wholesale Trade in, and Use of Opium, 1953, *UNTS*, Vol. 456, p. 3 (*Protocol on Poppy Plant, 1953*).

XLII. Single Convention on Narcotic Drugs, 1961, *UNTS*, Vol. 520, p. 151 (*Single Convention on Narcotic Drugs, 1961*).

XLIII. Convention on Road Traffic, with Annexes, 1949, *UNTS*, Vol. 125, p. 3 (*Convention on Road Traffic, 1949*).

XLIV. Protocol concerning Countries or Territories at present Occupied, 1949, *UNTS*, Vol. 125, p. 3 (*Protocol on Road Traffic, 1949*).

XLV. Protocol on Road Signs and Signals, 1949, *UNTS*, Vol. 182, p. 229 (*Protocol on Road Signs and Signals, 1949*).

XLVI. International Convention to Facilitate the Importation of Commercial Samples and Advertising Materials, 1952, *UNTS*, Vol. 221, p. 255 (*Convention on Commercial Samples, 1952*).

XLVII. Convention concerning Customs Facilities for Touring, 1954, *UNTS*, Vol. 276, p. 191 (*Convention on Customs Facilities, 1954*).

XLVIII. Additional Protocol to the Convention concerning Customs Facilities for Touring, relating to the Importation of Tourist Publicity Documents and Materials, 1954, *UNTS*, Vol. 276, p. 191 (*Protocol on Customs Facilities, 1954*).

XLIX. Customs Convention on the Temporary Importation of Private Road Vehicles, 1954, *UNTS*, Vol. 282, p. 249 (*Convention on the Importation Road Vehicles, 1954*).

L. Convention on Transit Trade of Land-Locked States, 1965, *TD/TRANSIT/9* (*Convention on Transit Trade, 1965*).

LI. International Convention relating to Economic Statistics, 1928, and amended by the Protocol, 1948, *UNTS*, Vol. 73, p. 39 (*Convention on Economic Statistics, 1928, amended by the 1948 Protocol*).

LII. Protocol for the further extension of the period of validity of the Convention on the Declaration of Death of Missing Persons, 1967, Text of the Convention, *UNTS*, Vol. 119, p. 99 (*Protocol Concerning the Declaration of Death of Missing Persons, 1967*).

LIII. Convention on the Recovery Abroad of Maintenance, 1956, *UNTS*, Vol. 268, p. 3 (*Convention on Maintenance, 1956*).

LIV. Convention on the Recognition and Enforcement of Foreign Arbitral Awards, 1958, *UNTS*, Vol. 330, p. 3 (*Convention on Foreign Arbitral Awards, 1958*).

LV. Revised General Act for the Pacific Settlement of International Disputes, 1949, *UNTS*, Vol 71, p. 101 (*Revised General Act, 1949*).

ANNEX V

LIST OF "LIMITED" MULTILATERAL TREATIES ADOPTED BY E.C.E., WITH SOURCES OF THE TEXTS OF TREATIES AND THE NUMBER OF EUROPEAN STATES PARTIES THERETO IN BRACKETS

1. European Agreement supplementing the 1949 Convention on Road Traffic and the 1949 Protocol on Road Signs and Signals, 1950, *UNTS*, Vol. 182, p. 286, (13).
2. European Agreement on the application of article 23 of the 1949 Convention on Road Traffic concerning the dimensions and weights of vehicles permitted to travel on certain roads of the Contracting Parties, 1950, *UNTS*, Vol. 133, p. 368, (7).
3. Declaration on the Construction of Main International Traffic Arteries, 1950, *UNTS*, Vol. 92, p. 91, (21).
4. General Agreement on Economic Regulations for International Road Transport, 1954, *E/ECE/186 (E/ECE/TRANS/460)*, (4).
5. Agreement on Signs and Road Works, amending the European Agreement of 16 September 1950 supplementing the 1949 Convention on Road Traffic and the 1949 Protocol on Road Signs and Signals, 1955, *E/ECE/223 (E/ECE/TRANS/481)*, (6).
6. Convention on the Taxation of Road Vehicles for Private Use in International Traffic, 1956, *UNTS*, Vol. 339, p. 3, (14).
7. Convention on the Contract for the International Carriage of Goods by Road (CMR), 1956, *UNTS*, Vol. 399, p. 189, (11).
8. Convention on the Taxation of Road Vehicles Engaged in International Goods Transport, 1956, *UNTS*, Vol. 436, p. 115, (9).
9. Convention on the Taxation of Road Vehicles Engaged in International Passenger Transport, 1956, *UNTS*, Vol. 436, p. 131, (11).

10. European Agreement concerning the International Carriage of Dangerpus Goods by Road (ADR), 1957, *E/ECE/322* (*E/ECE/ TRANS/503*), (6).
11. European Agreement on Road Markings, 1957, *UNTS*, Vol. 372, p. 159, (12).
12. Agreement concerning the Adoption of Uniform Conditions of Approval and Reciprocal Recognition of Approval for Motor Vehicle Equipment and Parts, 1958, *UNTS*, Vol. 335, p. 211, (11).
13. Agreement on Special Equipment for the Transport of Perishable Foodstuffs and on the Use of such Equipment for the International Transport of some of those Food Stuffs, 1962, *E/ECE/456* (*E/ECE/ TRANS/526*), (3).
14. European Agreement concerning the Work of Crews of Vehicles Engaged in International Road Transport (AETR), 1962, *E/ECE/ 457* (*E/ECE/TRANS/527*, (0).
15. Customs Convention on Containers, 1956, *UNTS*, Vol. 338, p. 103, (23).
16. Customs Convention on the Temporary Importation of Commercial Road Vehicles, 1956, *UNTS*, Vol. 327, p. 123, (22).
17. Customs Convention on the Temporary Importation for Private Use of Aircraft and Pleasure Boats, 1956, *UNTS*, Vol. 319, p. 21, (17).
18. Customs Convention concerning Spare Parts used for Repairing EUROP Wagons, *UNTS*, Vol. 383, p. 229, (9).
19. Customs Convention on the International Transport of Goods under Cover or TIR Carnets (TIR Convention), 1959, *UNTS*, Vol. 348, p. 13, (24).
20. European Convention on Customs Treatment of Pallets used in International Transport, *UNTS*, Vol. 429, p. 211, (19).
21. International Convention to Facilitate the Crossing of Frontiers for Passengers and Baggage carried by Rail, 1952, *UNTS*, Vol. 163, p. 3, (9).
22. International Convention to Facilitate the Crossing of Frontiers for Goods Carried by Rail, 1952, *UNTS*, Vol. 163, p. 27, (10).
23. Convention relating to the Unification of Certain Rules concerning Collisions in Inland Navigation, 1960, *UNTS*, Vol. 572, (5).
24. Convention on the Registration of Inland Navigation Vessels, 1965, (0).
25. Convention on the Measurement of Inland Navigation Vessels, 1966, *E/ECE/626* (*E/ECE/TRANS/546*), (0).
26. European Convention on International Commercial Arbitration, 1961, *UNTS*, Vol. 484, p. 349, (12).

ANNEX VI

RESOLUTION OF THE ASSEMBLY OF THE
LEAGUE OF NATIONS, 3 OCTOBER 1930

The Assembly:

Having examined with the greatest interest the report of the Committee appointed to consider the question of the ratification and signature of conventions concluded under the auspices of the League of Nations in accordance with an Assembly resolution of September 24th, 1929;

Being convinced that the solution of the problem of ratification depends to a great extent upon satisfactory preparation for the conferences which are convened to draw up conventions;

Considering it to be of the greatest importance that all steps should be taken to assure that conventions concluded under the auspices of the League of Nations should be accepted by the largest possible number of countries and that ratifications of such conventions should be deposited with the least possible delay:

Expresses its appreciation of the work of the Committee and its approval of their report; and

Recommends that effect should be given to the proposals contained in the report of the Committee in the manner set out in the immediately following resolutions.

I.

That each year the Secretary-General should request any Member of the League or non-Member State which has signed any general convention concluded under the auspices of the League of Nations but has not ratified it before the expiry of one year from the date at which the protocol of signature is closed, to inform him what are its intentions with regard to the ratification of the convention. Such requests of the Secretary-General to Governments should be sent at such a date in each year as to allow time for the replies of Governments to be received before the date of the Assembly, and information as to the requests so made and replies received should be communicated to the Assembly for its consideration.

II.

That, at such times and at such intervals as seem suitable in the circumstances, the Secretary-General should, in the case of each general convention concluded under the auspices of the League of Nations, request the Government of any Member of the League of Nations which has neither signed nor acceded to a convention within a period of five years from the date on which the convention became open for signature, to state its views with regard to the convention—in particular whether such Government considers there is any possibility of its accession to the convention or whether it has objections to the substance of the convention which prevent it from accepting the convention. Information of all such requests made by the Secretary-General and of all replies received should be communicated to the Assembly.

III.

That the Council of the League should, with regard to each existing general convention negotiated under the auspices of the League of Nations, consider, after consultation with any appropriate organ or committee of the League, and in the light of such information as may be available as to the result of the enquiries recommended in resolutions . . . and any other enquiries that the Council may think fit, whether it would be desirable and expedient that a second conference should be summoned for the purpose of determining whether amendments should be introduced into the convention or other means adopted, to facilitate the acceptance of the convention by a greater number of countries.

IV.

That, in the case of all general conventions to be negotiated under the auspices of the League of Nations, the following preparatory procedure should, in principle, be followed, exception made of the cases where previous conventions or arrangements have established a special procedure or where, owing to the nature of the questions to be treated or to special circumstances, the Assembly or the Council consider other methods to be more appropriate:

1. Where an organ of the League of Nations recommends the conclusion of a general convention on any matter, it shall prepare a memorandum explaining the objects which it is desired to achieve by the conclusion of the convention and the benefits which result therefrom. Such memorandum shall be submitted to the Council of the League of Nations.

2. If the Council approves the proposal in principle, a first draft convention shall be prepared and communicated, together with the explanatory memorandum, to Governments, with the request that, if they feel that the draft should be taken into consideration, they shall inform the Secretary-General of their views, both with regard to the main objects or the suggested means of attaining them, and also with regard to the draft convention. In some cases, it may be desirable to annex a specific questionnaire.

3. The draft convention and the observations of Governments (together with the answers to the questionnaire, if any) shall be communicated to the Assembly, and the Assembly shall then decide whether to propose to the Council to convoke the contemplated conference.

4. If the Assembly recommends that a conference should be convoked, the Council shall arrange for the preparation of a draft convention, in the light of the replies received from Governments and the new draft convention (together with the replies of other Governments) shall be transmitted to each Government, with a request for their opinion on the provisions of the draft and any observations on the above-mentioned replies of the other Governments.

5. In the light of the results of this second consultation of the Governments, the Council shall decide whether the conference should be convoked and fix the date.

6. The Council, in fixing the date for the convocation of a conference, shall endeavour, as far as possible, to avoid two League of Nations conferences being held simultaneously, and to ensure the lapse of a reasonable interval between two conferences.

7. The procedure set out in the preceding paragraphs will be followed as far as possible in the case of draft conventions, the desirability of which is recognized by a decision of the Assembly or as the result of a proposal by a Government.

The above rules shall be communicated to the technical organizations of the League of Nations and to the Governments, for the purpose of enabling the Assembly at its next session to consider whether changes should be made therein as a result of any suggestions which may be made.

V.

That, in conformity with the recommendations contained in Part III, paragraphs 2(d), (e) and (f), of the report of the Committee appointed in accordance with the resolution of the Assembly of September 24th, 1929 (see document A.10.1930.V), at future conferences held under the auspices of the League of Nations at which general conventions are signed, protocols of signature shall, as far as possible, be drawn up on the general lines of the alternative drafts set out in Annexes I and II of the present resolution.

ANNEX I [OF THE RESOLUTION]

Protocol of Signature

In signing the Convention of this day's date relating to . . . the undersigned plenipotentiaries, being duly authorised to this effect and in the name of their respective Governments, declare that they have agreed as follows:

I. That the Government of every Member of the League of Nations or non-Member State on whose behalf the said Convention has been signed undertakes, not later than . . . (date) either to submit the said Convention for parliamentary approval, or to inform the Secretary-General of the League of Nations of its attitude with regard to the Convention.

II. If on . . . (date) the said Convention is not in force with regard to . . . Members of the League of Nations and non-Member States, the Secretary-General of the League shall bring the situation to the attention of the Council of the League of Nations, which may either convene a new conference of all the Members of the League and non-Member States on whose behalf the Convention has been signed or accessions thereto deposited, to consider the situation, or take such other measures as it considers necessary. The Government of every signatory or acceding State undertakes to be represented at any conference so convened. The Governments of Members of the League and non-Member States which have not signed the Convention or acceded thereto may also be invited to be represented at any conference so convened by the Council of the League.

Note. The procedure provided for in this Annex is generally suitable for most general conventions. In cases in which it is applied, the final article of the convention should be drafted in the usual form and should not fix any named or final date for the entry into force of the convention, but should permit its entry into force on receipt of a relatively small number of ratifications or accessions.

ANNEX II [OF THE RESOLUTION]

Final Article of the Convention

Article X

The present Convention shall enter into force on . . . (date), provided that, on this date, ratifications or accessions have been deposited with or notified to the Secretary-General of the League of Nations on behalf of . . .[1] Members of the League of Nations or non-Member States.

---

[1] The figure indicated here should be a relatively large one.

Protocol of Signature.

In signing the Convention of to-day's date relating to . . . the undersigned plenipotentiaries, being duly authorised to this effect and in the name of their respective Governments, declare that they have agreed as follows:

If on . . .[2] the said Convention has not come into force in accordance with the provisions of Article X, the Secretary-General of the League of Nations shall bring the situation to the attention of the Council of the League of Nations, which may either convene a new conference of all the Members of the League and non-Member States on whose behalf the Convention has been signed or accessions thereto deposited to consider the situation, or take such other measures as it considers necessary. The Government of every signatory or acceding State undertakes to be represented at any conference so convened.

Note. The procedure provided for in Annex II is suitable for certain types of conventions whose practical utility depends on their immediate entry into force for a considerable number of States.

VI.

That the Council will investigate to what extent in the case of general conventions dealing with particular matters, it is possible—in view of the constitutional law and practices of different States—to adopt the procedure of signing instruments in the form of governmental agreements which are not subject to ratification, and that, to the extent that it is possible to do so, this procedure should be followed in regard to minor and technical matters.

VII.

That, in future, general conventions negotiated under the auspices of the League of Nations and made subject to ratification shall not be left open for signature after the close of the conference for a longer period than six months, unless special reasons render a longer period advisable.

[2] Same date as that indicated in art. X.

ANNEX VII

FUNCTIONS OF THE SECTION ON TREATY AFFAIRS (L/T) IN THE U.S. DEPARTMENT OF STATE*

1. Gives advice and assistance on all aspects of treaty law and procedure, including constitutional questions, drafting, negotiation, and interpretation of treaties, participation in Congressional hearings on treaty matters and international conferences where special questions of treaty law or drafting are involved.

2. Formulates and applies basic treaty policy through the Department's regulations on treaties to ensure that the making of treaties is carried out within constitutional and other appropriate limits and that the Secretary or his designee approves the negotiation and signature of each treaty or other international agreement of substance.

3. Prepares all formal presidential documents regarding treaties—full powers authorizing signature, instruments of ratification and proclamations of treaties—and the Secretary's report to the President and the President's message for the transmission of treaties to the Senate for its advice and consent to ratification.

4. Performs all procedural and depositary functions regarding treaties, such as arranging for and conducting all ceremonies of signing, and exchange or deposit of ratifications; passes upon full powers, ratifications, accessions, notices of termination and other documents submitted by other governments and assists other governments on all procedural matters in connection with treaties being made with them or for which the U.S. is depositary.

5. Publishes in the "Treaties and Other International Acts Series"

* This information was kindly furnished by the Department of State, the Government of the United States.

(TIAS) and in the annual volume of *United States Treaties and Other International Agreements* (UST) the texts of all treaties and other international agreements concluded by the United States; prepares other publications on treaties, such as the annual list of *Treaties in Force* and the 16 volume collection of treaty texts currently in preparation for the period 1776-1949; and compiles the information under Treaty Information in the weekly issues of the Department of State Bulletin, and texts of treaty provisions on various subjects, such as notification of consular officers of the arrest of their fellow nationals. Registers all such treaties and agreements with the United Nations and, where they relate to aviation, with the International Civil Aviation Organization.

6. Maintains Department's official register on treaties submitted to the Senate and analytical records on each treaty or agreement concluded for the U.S., including background studies, negotiations, signature, entry into force, application, amendments and terminations; maintains, so far as practicable, information on treaties and other agreements concluded between other countries. . . .

INDEX

177

Secretariat, 17
  Arabic Unit in, 92
  Department of Public Information,
    15
  dissemination of information by,
    62-65
  succession and, 132-34
  procedures and assistance, 145-
    46
Trusteeship Council, 55
United Nations Juridical Yearbook,
    63
United Nations Monthly Chronicle,
    64
United Nations Yearbook, 63
*United Nations Yearbook on Human
    Rights,* 63
United States of America
  agreements in simplified form in,
    130*n*
  constitutional limitations on treaties
    in, 110-13
  drafting of implementing legislation
    in, 83
  form of legislative approval in, 116-
    17
  legislative controls over treaty con-
    clusion in, 94, 101
  postponement of acceptances by,
    82
  reservations made by, 153
Universal Declaration of Human Rights,
    21, 118
  translation of, 92
UNWRA, 21*n*
Upper Volta, 97*n*, 99*n*
  succession and, 136*n*, 138, 139,
    142, 143
Uruguay, 47*n*, 103*n*
Urrutia, Francisco, 8

Venezuela, 47*n*, 103
  Constitution of, 107
  reservations made by, 149*n*, 150*n*,
    152*n*, 153
Vienna Convention on Consular Re-
    lations (1963), 10*n*, 29, 30, 150

forms of acceptance prescribed in,
    121
  promotion of, 46*n*
  tempo of acceptance of, 38
Vienna Convention on Diplomatic Re-
    lations (1961), 10*n*, 29, 30
  forms of acceptance prescribed in,
    121
  implementing legislation on, 83-84,
    96-97, 111-12
  promotion of, 42, 46*n*
  reservations to, 150
  succession to, 134
  tempo of acceptance of, 38
  translation of, 91
Vienna Convention on the Law of
    Treaties (1969), 10, 12-13,
    131
  article regarding reservations in,
    148-49
Vietnam, Republic of, 25*n*, 150*n*

Weis, Paul, 8
Western European States, 28
  See also specific States
Western Samoa, 25*n*, 27*n*, 94*n*
  succession and, 137-39, 141*n*
Wilcox, Francis, 54*n*
*Work of the International Law Com-
    mission, The* (U.N. Study),
    146
World Health Organization
  Constitution of, 123n
  reporting by States to, 62
World Refugee Year, 45-46

Yasseen, Mustafa Kamil, 8
Yemen, 97*n*
Yugoslavia, 47*n*, 53, 127, 153

Zambia, 94*n*
  succession and, 134*n*, 136*n*, 137*n*,
    138*n*, 140*n*, 141*n*, 142*n*
Zanzibar, 139, 142
  See also Tanzania